Literature and Composition

English 2

Third Edition

Janice Campbell

Everyday Education
Making Time for Things That Matter
www.Everyday-Education.com

Excellence in Literature: Reading and Writing through the Classics
Introduction to Literature (English I)
Literature and Composition (English II)
American Literature: A Survey Course (English III)
British Literature: A Survey Course (English IV)
World Literature: A Survey Course (English V)

Third Edition: © 2014 Everyday Education, LLC

Everyday Education, LLC
P.O. Box 549
Ashland, VA 23005
www.Everyday-Education.com

Front Cover Art: *The Priest* by Bernardo Ferrándiz, c. 1885

Campbell, Janice
Literature and composition/ Excellence in literature: reading and writing through the classics / Janice Campbell

ISBN: 978-1-61322-024-5

1. Literature—Explication. 2. Literature—History and Criticism. 3. Books and reading. I. Title.

It is a great thing to start life with a small number of

really good books

which are your very own.

You may not appreciate them at first.

You may pine for your novel of crude and unadulterated adventure.

You may, and will, give it the preference when you can.

But the dull days come, and the rainy days come,

and always you are driven to fill up the chinks of your reading

with the worthy books which wait so patiently for your notice.

And then suddenly, on a day which marks an epoch in your life,

you understand the difference.

You see, like a flash, how the one stands for nothing,

and the other for literature.

From that day onwards you may return to your crudities,

but at least you do so with some

standard of comparison in your mind.

You can never be the same as you were before.

Then gradually the good thing becomes more dear to you;

it builds itself up with your growing mind;

it becomes a part of your better self, and so,

at last, you can look, as I do now, at the old covers

and love them for all that they have meant in the past.

—Arthur Conan Doyle, *Through the Magic Door*

Thank you!

I would like to offer special thanks to some of my former students,
who graciously agreed to share their work as models.

Erin Bensing

Jonathan Bensing

Eric Lansing

Rebecca Shealy-Houghton

Jesse Thompson

I would also like to thank

Rebecca Shealy-Houghton- Research Assistant and Website Editor

Craig Campbell- Music and Historical Context Consultant

Maria Gerber- IEW Project Manager

*Blessing, and glory, and wisdom, and thanksgiving, and honour, and power,
and might, be unto our God for ever and ever. Amen.*

Revelation 7:12 KJV

Deo gratias.

Contents

Introduction

Dear Student,

Do you know that very few people know how to read?

It is not that they cannot decipher words on a page, but they simply do not know how to place what they read into its proper literary and historical context. They may understand WHAT happened in a story, but they do not know WHY. They may feel strongly about the story, yet they never stop to wonder WHY they feel as they do, or HOW the author made it happen.

If you are wondering why you should care about the HOW and WHY of literature, think about it like this: Reading without understanding is like walking onto a softball field and batting the ball, without any knowledge of what to do next. You may hit the ball out of the park, but if you do not run the bases and complete the play, you have missed the whole point of the activity.

It is the same with reading. In order to complete the process, it is necessary to think analytically about what you read. Reading is a conversation between a reader and a writer. The author creates a world, peoples it with characters, and presents a story. The reader enters the author's world, meets the characters, and follows the story line. When you write about literature, as you will this year, the conversation shifts. It becomes a dialogue between you, as an analytical reader and writer, and the reader of your essay.

In this literature curriculum, I will introduce you to a technique I call "deep reading." As you work through each assigned story, you will also learn about the historic, literary, and artistic context in which the story was written. I will give you the opportunity and resources to discover more about the story, the author, and the various elements of the text, including plot, setting, characterization, and more. This will help you make sense of each great book and will make the story more enjoyable.

You will find that you like some books and authors better than others, just as I do. Each novel, poem, essay, or play in this literature series has been carefully chosen for its quality and its place in the panorama of literary history. Even if you find you do not enjoy a particular work as much as another, it has been included because it has something important to convey. One thing you will discover is that sometimes the stories you like least stick with you the longest and sometimes even teach you the most.

I love to read, and I am happy to have the opportunity to share some of my favorite great books with you. Some will make you laugh, others may make you cry, but above all, I hope they make you think. When you finish your reading for the year, I know that your mind will be more richly furnished than when you began, and that is a very good thing.

Janice Campbell

www.ExcellenceInLiterature.com

P. S. As you read through this book, you will most likely encounter words you do not know. I am sure you know what to do when this happens. Look it up and write down the word and its definition, and you will be expanding your vocabulary without much effort at all.

Overview and Objectives

Excellence in Literature (EIL) is a college-preparatory course of study. It is my goal to

- Introduce students to great literature from the Western literary tradition.
- Teach students to read with discernment.
- Train independent, self-motivated learners.
- Provide tools students can use to strengthen their writing skills.
- Introduce students to sources for high-quality online and offline research.
- Prepare students for college classes by expecting carefully researched, well-considered material to be presented in standard format, with preliminary proofreading completed.

In the five levels of this literature series, you will be reading some of the greatest works of literature ever written. They are great not just because they are technically well done, though that certainly is a factor, but also because they reveal truth through the power of story.

EIL uses great literature, studied in its historic, literary, and artistic contexts, to help you learn to think and write analytically. This book is designed for students to use independently, so it contains specific instructions for each assignment, and a suggested schedule, as well as the references you need in order to do the background reading and research for each module.

You may be surprised to find I have not provided a lengthy introduction and a lot of background material for each book and author. This is because you have reached the age when you can assume responsibility for learning. Rather than spoon-feeding you basic, easily researched information (and having you zone out in the middle of paragraph two), I have provided resources and links that will enable you to perform the contextual research needed to fully understand the focus text. This is the kind of research you will be doing for college courses, so if you learn how to do it now, you should be quite good at it by the time you graduate!

How to Benefit from This Guide

To gain the greatest possible benefit from your literature study, you are responsible for reading this entire guide. Read the sections before and after the modules before you start working on the assignments. In the first section, you will find an explanation of how EIL works, suggestions for how to create a study routine and organize your study materials, chapters on how to read analytically and how to write essays. Following this you will find the syllabus section, with a study outline and schedule for each module. In the final section you will find instructions for writing specific types of papers, information for your writing mentor on how to evaluate papers, and sample papers that demonstrate correct MLA format (if you do not know what that is, be patient—it is explained in the samples and the glossary). Be sure to read all the chapters so you can be successful as you work through the assignments.

Each level of EIL has nine modules. Each module is intended to be completed in four relatively brief, but intense, weeks, though your writing mentor may decide to spend more or less time on a particular module. You may choose to group the modules into a traditional nine-month school year, or to use a four weeks on, one week off schedule. For a weekly routine, our family loosely followed a college-style block schedule in which we studied the humanities (literature, history, art, and music) in 2- to 3 hour blocks of time on Tuesday and Thursday; and math, science, and related subjects on Monday and Wednesday, but you are free to do what works best for you and your family.

Each assignment has been carefully chosen and scheduled so that knowledge and skills can build cumulatively, even if your writing mentor changes the order in which you study the modules. It is important that you learn time management skills that will help you complete assignments with minimal stress. If you are working with a writing mentor such as your parent, a writing evaluator, a coach, or a co-op

Excellence in Literature: Reading and Writing through the Classics

instructor, be sure to agree in advance on a schedule, so that you can plan your work efficiently. Above all, do not spend three weeks procrastinating; then try to cram the assigned reading and writing into one week. Believe me, it does not work!

Course Format

Excellence in Literature courses are designed to focus in depth on selected great authors or literary movements, while exploring the context of the author's life and work through additional reading and writing. This offers opportunity to practice writing in a number of different formats, as well as the opportunity to grow thoroughly familiar with some of the greatest writers and literary works of all time.

Audio Books

Although many students are visual learners and do well reading each novel, auditory[1] or kinesthetic learners may benefit from listening to unabridged versions of the more challenging works. Epic poems such as *Beowulf* or *Paradise Lost* work especially well in audio, as it becomes easier to appreciate the rhythm and cadence of the language. The goal is for you to thoroughly understand and enjoy the material we cover, so use the learning tools that work best for you.

Context Materials

For each module there will be additional material to read, listen to, or watch. These resources are designed to provide contextual information that will help you understand the focus work. These context resources include links to interesting and informative websites, and recommendations for additional readings. Many of these are hosted or linked at Excellence-in-Literature.com.

Do not feel limited by these resource suggestions. I encourage you to find and include other resources, such as videos, field trips, or other useful books. The more rich and varied the context materials, the more vivid and interesting the focus text will seem. If you find a book or author you particularly enjoy, take the time to read more of his or her writings or broaden your research. EIL is a solid foundation, and it is designed to be flexible, so you can shape it to reflect your own interests.

Study Clusters

You may want to consider planning the high school years in study clusters—grouping American history with American literature, British history with British

---

[1]An auditory learner is one who learns best by hearing; a kinesthetic learner learns by doing.

literature, and so forth. This reinforces learning and increases memorable context for both literature and history. You may mix and match EIL modules to fit the history you are studying.

The Honors Track

In each module, you will find additional reading suggestions under the "Honors" heading. If you would like to earn an honors-level grade (weighted by .5 grade point), you need to read an extra book and do an approach paper for each module. At the end of the school year, you will also write an additional research paper, which is assigned in the Honors chapter. This will complete the honors track.

To earn advanced placement or college credit for the class (weighted by 1.0 grade point), you will also need to take an AP or CLEP exam. You can find complete details on how to assign weighted grades and record advanced classes in my book, *Transcripts Made Easy* (www.TranscriptsMadeEasy.com). Additional information about how and why to earn college credits can be found in *Get a Jump Start on College!* (www.GetAJumpStartOnCollege.com).

Prerequisites for Success

Excellence in Literature is intended for use by students in grades 8–12. For each level, you are expected to have age-appropriate skills in grammar, spelling, and language mechanics. Students should grammar- and spell-check all papers before turning them in, as learning to self-edit is part of the writing process.

If you have not done literary analysis or essay writing, there are two resources I recommend. *Teaching the Classics with Worldview Supplement* by Adam Andrews is a brief DVD-based course that teaches literary analysis using short works to illustrate the principles and methods. For essay writing, *The Elegant Essay Writing Lessons* by Lesha Myers is the best resource I have seen. Both are published by the Institute for Excellence in Writing, and both can be used concurrently with *Excellence in Literature*.

Is it better to own or to borrow books?

I have discovered that if you have books in your home, they will be read. I do not expect you to purchase all the resources I have referenced, but I hope you will consider having a few of the most important on hand. You can find them used at online retailers such as Amazon.com or Alibris. com, or you may even be able to get them free through PaperbackSwap.com (you may use my referral, "readbx"). I have purchased many books quite cheaply from library sales, thrift shops, and yard sales. Studies have shown that the number of books owned in a family has a direct relationship to the student's long-term academic success, with measurably higher test scores for book owners than for age mates with fewer books in the home.

For the focus texts, I encourage you to consider purchasing nice, annotated paperback editions because those books will become part of your student's mental furniture and may be read and reread many times. For most of the books, my favorite editions are Modern Library Press Paperback Classics. You can find links to most of the recommended texts at Excellence-in-Literature.com.

Learning Philosophy

Learn (lûrn) v. 1 To acquire knowledge of or skill in by observation, study, instruction, etc. 2 To find out; ascertain: to learn the facts. 3 To memorize. 4 To acquire by or as by practice: to learn good habits.
—Webster Illustrated Contemporary Dictionary: Encyclopedic Edition 1971

The foundation of the *Excellence in Literature* philosophy is the verb "learn." I believe the acquisition of knowledge and skills is an active endeavor. The process of learning is focused within one person—the learner. Just as an infant makes the transition from being fed to feeding himself, a student who wants to be successful will begin to take an active role in absorbing and understanding information that will help him interpret his world. Although many students wait until college to make this transition, high school is actually an ideal time to learn how to learn.

As a writer, my goal is to impart not only knowledge, but also the tools and skills you need to take an active part in the learning process. I have always been a reader and an active learner, and I know from experience that the process is fascinating and invigorating. If you are an active learner, you will rarely be bored, and you can be confident in your ability to learn and do almost anything. There is great joy in learning, and this, above all, is what I want to communicate.

The Learning Process: Roles of Excellence in Literature, the Student, and the Writing Mentor

The EIL guide will

- Establish the scope and sequence for the class.
- Assign appropriate readings.
- Provide a suggested schedule for assignments.
- Provide time management and organization tips.
- Provide a rubric for objectively evaluating completed assignments.

The Student will

- Study this book and understand the sequence and timing of assignments.
- Ask questions of the writing mentor when something is not clearly understood.
- Actively seek to learn from each assignment.
- Complete all assignments on time.
- Make no excuses.
- Enjoy great literature.

The Writing Mentor (usually the parent) will

Help the student obtain required books and reference materials.

- Verify that assignments are completed on schedule.
- Use the rubric or select a qualified writing evaluator to provide feedback for the student.
- Provide an evaluation summary for the year, using the form found at the end of this book.

*Note: Week 3 assignments and those marked with an asterisk have instructions and a model for imitation. See Formats and Models chapter for details. Module "Introduction" includes "Something to think about . . ." and "Be sure to notice . . ." paragraphs.

Excellence in Literature Pacing Chart

Suggested pacing of modules: Move through nine modules per school year, adapting your pace as needed.

WEEK	What to Read	What to Write	Module Focus	Optional Honors Reading	Optional Honors Writing
1	Module 2.1 Introduction, *Robinson Crusoe* and Context Resources	Author Profile*	Spiritual autobiography; how real events can shape a novel	*The Swiss Family Robinson* / *The Further Adventures of Robinson Crusoe; Additional options*	
2		Short article or deserted island exercise			
3		Write a first draft and turn in for feedback.			Approach Paper*
4		Edit and revise assignment; turn in.			
5	Module 2.2 Introduction, *Walden* and Context Resources	Author Profile*	Transcendentalist movement; characteristics of Romanticism	"Civil Disobedience" and "Self-Reliance"	
6		Letter or Historical Period/Event Approach Paper*			
7		Write a first draft and turn in for feedback.			Approach Paper*
8		Edit and revise assignment; turn in.			
9	Module 2.3 Introduction, *The Count of Monte Cristo*, and Context Resources	Author Profile*	Example of early historical fiction; life in 19th-century France	*The Man in the Iron Mask* or *The Three Musketeers*	
10		Approach Paper* or graphic storyline			
11		Write a first draft and turn in for feedback.			Approach Paper*
12		Edit and revise essay; turn in.			
13	Module 2.4 Introduction, *Heart of Darkness* and Context Resources	Author Profile*	Framed narrative; colonialism	*Manalive*	
14		Historical Period/Event Approach Paper*			
15		Write a first draft and turn in for feedback.			Approach Paper*
16		Edit and revise essay; turn in.			

*Note: Assignments marked with an asterisk have a model for imitation. See Formats and Models chapter for details.

Excellence in Literature Pacing Chart

Suggested Pacing of Modules: *Move through nine modules each school year, adapting your pace as needed.*

WEEK	What to Read	What to Write	Module Focus	Optional Honors Reading	Optional Honors Writing
17	Module 2.5 Introduction, *Till we Have Faces*, and Context Resources	Author Profile*	Unreliable narrator; discernment		
18		Rewrite the legend in a modern setting			
19		Write a first draft and turn in for feedback.		*The Screwtape Letters*	
20		Edit and revise assignment; turn in.			Approach Paper*
21	Module 2.6 Introduction, *Death Comes for the Archbishop*, and Context Resources	Author Profile*	Vivid setting; characteristics of regional and episodic fiction		
22		Descriptive paper in Cather's style			
23		Write a first draft and turn in for feedback.		*Country of the Pointed Firs*	
24		Edit and revise essay; turn in.			Approach Paper*
25	Module 2.7 Introduction, Context Resources, and *Julius Caesar*	Author Profile*	Use of irony and rhetoric		
26		Scene summaries; copy speeches			
27		Write a first draft and turn in for feedback.		*King John*	
28		Edit and revise assignment; turn in.			Approach Paper*
29	Module 2.8 Introduction, *Ivanhoe*, and Context Resources	Author Profile*	Early historical fiction; illustrating virtue in action		
30		Approach Paper*			
31		Write a first draft and turn in for feedback.		*Merchant of Venice* or *Rob Roy*	
32		Edit and revise assignment; turn in.			Approach Paper*

33	Module 2.9 Introduction, *The Importance of Being Earnest*, and Context Resources	Author Profile*	
34		Retell as a short story	Conventions of farce; use of absurdity
35		Write a first draft and turn in for feedback.	*Kim*
36		Edit and revise assignment; turn in.	Approach Paper*

Getting Started

Before you begin, set up a study area and English notebook to help you stay organized. If you learn how to do this now, you will be a step ahead when you get to college and realize that you are completely responsible for creating a time and place to learn. College professors usually hand out a syllabus at the first class, with all the assignments and due dates for the semester. They do not remind you of what is coming up, so if you do not have a method for keeping on top of everything, you can quickly fall behind. You will find the organizational techniques you learn from EIL helpful for any class you take in the future.

What belongs in a study area?

Study area basics are a comfortable chair, bright light, your English notebook and reading log, calendar or datebook, good dictionary, thesaurus, writer's handbook, pens, pencils, paper, sticky notes such as Post-it® notes, and possibly a computer. Being organized will make your study time more pleasant and productive, so be sure to start the school year by pulling together these things.

How to Use Items in Your Study Area

Chair and light: Read here (see the chapter on "How to Read a Book"). You want to be comfortable enough to enjoy the experience, but not so comfortable that you fall asleep. It is pleasant to read near a window, but you should also have a reading light positioned so that the light falls on your book. If you find that your eyes get tired quickly, you may need a brighter light or even reading glasses. Do not hesitate to get your eyes checked, so you can enjoy reading.

Calendar: Use a calendar or planner to record assignment deadlines, field trips, and other activities. At the beginning of each module, check the number of pages in your focus text and number of context resources; then plan how many you need to read daily in order to finish the focus text before you begin the essay.

English notebook: Organize your English papers in a three-ring binder. You can use page protectors that hold two sheets back-to-back, or you can punch holes and put everything directly into the binder. The first thing you should see when you open the cover is a list of modules and assignments (look for the form right after the evaluation summary). Next, put in a copy of each assignment you do, along with your note pages and the evaluation rubrics you receive. You may want to have a glossary section at the end with lists of new words you have learned, so you can review them easily.

Reading log: List everything you read—not just the books you read for English, but everything. Write the title, author, a one- or two-sentence summary of the book, and a comment or rating. A blank journal is handy for this, or you may prefer to keep the record in a database on your computer. There is even a form in my book, *Transcripts Made Easy*, that you can reproduce and use.

Dictionary: Look up unfamiliar words you encounter. If you can guess their meaning from the context, just write down the word on a small sticky note and stick it on the page. Look it up after you are finished reading. If you cannot guess the meaning from the context, look it up before continuing. Looking up challenging words not only builds vocabulary and helps you remember the word, but also reveals the nuances in meaning that set the word apart from its synonyms. My favorite dictionary is the *Oxford Shorter English Dictionary* because most of the word usage examples are from literature, but most college dictionaries are acceptable as well.

Thesaurus: Use this when you find yourself repeating the same descriptive words over and over. I use *Roget A to Z*, which is organized alphabetically. The English language is fascinating, and there is a perfect word for almost any occasion—please find it and use it!

EIL Handbook for Writers, Writers Inc., or other handbook: Cannot remember when to use a comma or a semicolon? Here is where you go to find out. Need instructions for how to write an expository essay? You will find it in your writer's handbook. A professional writer or editor always has several frequently used handbooks nearby. Writer's handbooks are packed with great information, and the reason professionals have several is that different handbooks have different areas of focus. No matter how competent you are as a writer, there is no way you can remember every tiny detail of grammar, style, or usage, so it pays to check your handbook—chances are, you will find exactly the help you need.

Pens: Use a pen for mind mapping (thinking on paper) rough drafts, illustrations, Venn diagrams, and more. When I was in college, one of my favorite ways to study a long, challenging work was to use an 18" x 24" sketch pad and multi colored gel pens. I spent one semester in an in-depth independent study of Edmund Spenser's *The Fairie Queene* and found that the best way to see themes and remember what happened where was to summarize each book of the poem with a quick sketch and bullet points illustrating each canto.

Pencils: These are for writing in your books. Yes, I mean it—I want you to underline key passages, talk back to the characters, note thoughts that occur to you as you read, and so forth. This is called annotation, and it is part of active reading (you will read more about this in the "How to Read a Book" chapter). Taking notes in the text will help you get the most out of a story. If you have to use library books for your focus texts, you will not be able to annotate as easily, but you can put a piece of paper in the back of the book and use it for the things you would normally write in the book.

Sticky notes: One of the first things to do is to make sticky-note tabs for your writer's handbook. This helps you turn quickly to key pages. For classes using an anthology, I recommend that at the beginning of the semester you look at the syllabus and go through the anthology and place a sticky-note tab with the author's last name and the title of the work beside each assigned piece. This saves time and helps remind you of what you have covered, and what remains.

Computer: When you reach college or the business world, you will need to know how to use a computer, so high school is the time to become comfortable with its basic functions. Rather than using a word-processing program on your computer, I suggest learning to use the free online word-processing program by Google. It is accessible through any Internet-connected computer, and your paper can be easily shared with a writing instructor, no matter where he or she is located.

Computer Tips

Formatting papers: Once you are in high school, all written work should be submitted in a college-style format. This means it should be typed in Times New Roman or a similar font, double-spaced, with one-inch margins all around (see the sample paper in the back of this book). Be sure to have the grammar- and spell-check turned on in your word processing program, but do not rely too heavily on these checking tools, because they are often wrong. Always do a "human proofread" by reading your paper aloud to yourself before turning it in. Reading aloud helps you slow down enough to spot typos and hear sentences or phrases that do not flow smoothly.

One space after terminal punctuation: Space only once after any terminal punctuation (period, question mark, etc.). Old typing instruction books used to require two spaces after terminal punctuation because typewriters use what is called a mono-spaced type, and the double spacing helped the eye distinguish the end of a sentence. Computer fonts are proportionally spaced, and proper spacing is programmed in. Double spacing creates unattractive blobs of white down a page and is a dead giveaway that outdated methods are being used.

Saving your document: Always create a computer folder for each class, and use a descriptive file name when you save your papers. For example, if you are writing the essay on Benjamin Franklin's *Autobiography* from the first module of American Literature, name the file "eil3-u1-franklin," and it will be easy to find anytime you need it.

If a paper gets "lost" on your computer: If you are new to the world of computers, you may occasionally think you have lost something on your computer. If you have been typing and your text seems to disappear, try pressing the Command key along with Z. This is the "undo" command, and it will undo the last thing you did, which should bring your paper back into view. If it does not, you can search your hard drive for the file name you used when you saved it. If you are using a Mac computer or Google Docs, any document should easily be found.

Frequently Asked Questions

Be curious always! For knowledge will not acquire you; you must acquire it.

—Sudie Back

If you have questions about any aspect of the curriculum or about studying in general, you may find the answers in this chapter.

Are all assignment instructions contained in this book?

This EIL guide contains the outline of the course, an assignment schedule for each module, models of the type of papers you will be writing, and evaluation information. In addition, you will need a copy of each of the novel-length focus works and a writer's handbook.

It is helpful to have old editions of the *Norton Anthologies* of American, British, and World Literature for additional information and other readings from the historic and literary context of each of the EIL focus works. In addition, you will need access to standard study and reference tools as listed in the "Getting Started" chapter.

You do not tell me how many pages to read each day. How will I know?

It is all about time management! This is a college-prep class, so you will be learning to look ahead and pace yourself. For modules based upon a novel-length work, you have a couple of options: 1) Sit down the first day and read the whole book in several hours; then use the rest of the time to gather supporting information; perhaps read another book by the author; and write your essay; or 2) Divide the book into two equal parts, and read one part per week, leaving the last two weeks to write and polish your essay. I prefer the first method, as the story is usually more interesting if it is not read in tiny fragments over a long period of time. This also leaves plenty of time to draft, revise, and polish your essay.

C. S. Lewis wrote that "a narrative style is not to be judged by snippets. You must read for at least half a day and read with your mind on the story" (from *English Literature in the Sixteenth Century Excluding Drama*). He is a wise guide, because immersion changes the experience of reading from an assignment to a journey into another world, another place, and another time. Whatever you do, start reading the first day of the module, and read every day until the book is finished. Do not procrastinate. And do not forget your context readings!

Can I use library books, or do I have to buy them?

I encourage active reading that includes annotation, especially of the focus works. This means underlining and making notes in the margin, and librarians really hate that. So I recommend you buy the focus books. You can probably find used copies fairly cheaply.

Do you recommend a particular edition of each book?

It is important to have books that are pleasant to hold and read so that you enjoy the process and do not suffer from eyestrain. I do not recommend mass-market paperbacks, since they usually have too-small type, very small margins, and no scholarly introduction or discussion questions. Many are so hard to hold open that the spine is soon broken.

My favorite editions include Modern Library Paperback Classics. Norton, Penguin, and Oxford. The newest editions from these publishers are designed to lie open like a hardback, and they usually have insightful introductions and good discussion questions at the end. You will find links to each of my recommended editions on the Excellence-in-Literature.com site.

Can I read the focus texts on an e-reader?

You can read the texts on an e-reader such as the Kindle® or Nook®, but it is not always easy to annotate as you are reading or to page back to look up a character or event. In addition, if you use free versions from the public domain, be aware that the available translations may not be of the best quality. If you decide to use an e-reader, be sure to learn how to highlight and add notes and bookmarks.

The assignment said to write a 500-word essay. I accidentally wrote 603 words. What shall I do?

You can edit to make your work tighter, which will usually make your paper better. As Strunk and White admonish in *Elements of Style*, it is best to "omit needless words." The second option is to not worry about it. The word count is a minimum rather than a maximum requirement. It is stated as number of words rather than number of pages so that teachers will not receive essays with 16-point type and 2" margins, because someone had to fill three pages and had no ideas. Word count allows no fudging.

What should go into the assignment header?

Every paper you turn in should have a proper heading as shown in the sample papers in the Formats and Models chapter. The heading should include your first and last name, the class name with the instructor's name on the same line, the date, and the essay prompt. The essay prompt is included to make it easy for the evaluator to determine whether your essay is on topic, and it is especially important for modules in which you have a choice of topics.

How do I download and print items from the Internet?

If you have done some Internet research, or if I have provided a link or URL to a resource you need to download and print, you can follow these steps:

1. Copy (control + c) the entire underlined URL, and paste (control + v) it into the address window of your browser, and click "enter."

2. If the page that appears offers a link to a printable copy, click the link to print directly from the screen.

3. If there is no link to a printable copy, hold down the left button of your mouse, and drag to select the text you want to copy.

4. Copy and paste the text into a blank TextEdit or Notepad file, and save it to your English folder or to your Evernote.com account online.

5. Go back to the web page where you found the information. Select the URL in the address line, and copy and paste it at the end of your text. Type in the date you accessed the website and any other information you think may be important. You may need some of this information for your Works Cited page. Remember that it is never okay to copy material from anywhere and turn it in as your own work.

Why are there a lot of Internet resources?

First, they are free and globally available. If you do not have a computer with Internet access, chances are that you can use one at your local library or at a friend's house. Second, you need to know how to use a computer responsibly, and how to find the kind of resources you will need for the future, whether that future involves college, business, or teaching your own children. My goal is to introduce you to a lot of useful sites and resources, and to make you aware of what is available. As an ongoing project, we have begun to host many of these resources at our own Excellence-in-Literature.com website, so they will always be easily available.

What happens if a link does not work?

The Internet is an ever-changing place, so if a link is not on our website, there is a chance it will change. I have tried to choose resources from stable sources, so link moves should not be a major problem. If you type in a link and do not reach the resource, check to see if the resource is available on the Excellence-in-Literature.com website, categorized under "Resources" for your book level.

If you do not see the link on EIL, double-check each character you have typed, and make sure it exactly matches the link provided. If you are using an e-book and you copy and paste the link, be sure not to pick up any punctuation near the link because that will keep it from working.

Finally, if you are sure you have typed the link correctly, and you are not getting to the page, try doing a Google search for some of the keywords in the resource. For example, if the link for the Mark Twain House and Museum does not work, type "mark twain house museum" into the Google search box, and the correct resource should come up in the results. If it does not, you can try different combinations of keywords from the link description.

Do I have to read everything?

There are two things you absolutely must read, and they are this entire guide and each of the focus texts. I would like for you to read most of the context materials, but in a few cases there are more than you need. I have often included more than one suggested biography, simply because there are several good ones to choose from, and you may pick whichever one is easily available. The goal is for you to learn what you need to know in order to understand the author and the text and to write a thoughtful essay, not to just check off a random bunch of stuff.

I thought this was English class. Why do I have to look at art and listen to music?

Literature is a unique representation of its culture. Each great work was written by an author who was influenced by books, people, art, music, and events of his day. These influences, coupled with the author's education and family life, shaped the worldview that is inevitably reflected in his work.

In order to think intelligently about a poem, play, or story, you need to understand a bit about the author and his or her worldview. There is no easier or better way to do it than by sampling the art and music he or she might have seen or heard. The sights and sounds of an era can also help to illuminate the pervasive worldview that framed the focus text. You can think of content exploration as a virtual field trip!

How much time will EIL take each day?

The amount of time you spend depends on the length of the focus text. As an average, plan to spend at least one hour per day reading or writing about the focus text. Separate context reading or vocabulary work may add an additional 20–45 minutes per day.

Our family is different—do we have to follow the schedule exactly as it is written?

The schedule I have provided is the one my students followed when I taught these courses online (which I no longer do). It works efficiently and will help you cover a lot of material over the course of the school year. However, I completely understand that every family is unique. You may change the schedule, drop a module, take two years to cover the book, or alter it in any way that will help it better serve your family.

If you are teaching EIL in a co-op or school, you have the same liberty, though students who are following along in the book can probably be counted on to remind you that "That's not what Mrs. Campbell said to do!" Whatever you do, I promise that the EIL Enforcement Department will *not* stop by to rap your knuckles. The curriculum is here to serve you, and I want you to enjoy using it.

Why read old books?

There are many reasons to read old books, but author and apologist C.S. Lewis simply suggests that it is necessary in order to "keep the clean sea breeze of the centuries blowing through our minds" in order to escape the "characteristic blindness of the twentieth century." He writes:

It is a good rule, after reading a new book, never to allow yourself another new one till you have read an old one in between. If that is too much for you, you should at least read one old one to every three new ones.

Every age has its own outlook. It is specially good at seeing certain truths and specially liable to make certain mistakes. We all, therefore, need the books that will correct the characteristic mistakes of our own period. And that means the old books. All contemporary writers share to some extent the contemporary outlook—even those, like myself, who seem most opposed to it . . . The only palliative is to keep the clean sea breeze of the centuries blowing through our minds, and this can be done only by reading old books . . . Two heads are better than one, not because either is infallible, but because they are unlikely to go wrong in the same direction. (From an introduction by C.S. Lewis to a translation of *Athanasius: On the Incarnation*. Read the entire essay online at http://www.spurgeon.org/~phil/history/ath-inc.htm.)

In another good essay on this topic, Professor Dominic Manganiello, D.Phil., explains to his students, "We will read old books, then, because in the past lie the foundations of our present and future hope. We will discover that the writings of the masters deal with 'primal and conventional things . . . the hunger for bread, the love of woman, the love of children, the desire for immortal life.'" The remainder of this essay can be found at http://www.augustinecollege.org/papers/DM_7Sept98.htm.

Finally, in perhaps the most compelling reason of all, Alexandr Solzhenitsyn pointed out that "literature conveys irrefutable condensed experience in yet another invaluable direction; namely, from generation to generation. Thus it becomes the living memory of the nation. Thus it preserves and kindles within itself the flame of her spent history, in a form which is safe from deformation and slander. In this way literature, together with language, protects the soul of the nation." You may read his entire 1970 Nobel Lecture at http://www.nobelprize.org/nobel_prizes/literature/laureates/1970/solzhenitsyn-lecture.html.

How to Read a Book

Some books are meant to be tasted, some swallowed, and some few digested . . .

—Francis Bacon

No, you have not picked up the wrong course by mistake—this is indeed high school English! I know you have been reading for years, but I want you to learn to read actively and analytically. I will review the basics of reading fiction and poetry here, so that you will have an idea of how to read and analyze throughout each of the Excellence in Literature courses.

If you are using any level of EIL and you have not thoroughly studied literary analysis, I recommend going through Adam Andrews' excellent *Teaching the Classics* DVD course, including the *Worldview Supplement*. This brief course uses short pieces of literature to teach the fundamentals of literary interpretation and analysis, and the Supplement teaches how to analyze literature from a worldview perspective. This course is brief enough that it can be used over the summer before you begin EIL, or even concurrently.

If you are studying English III, IV, or V, I also recommend reading the books by James W. Sire and Gene Edward Veith or Mortimer Adler and Charles Van Doren (see details of these recommendations in the Resources chapter). Sire and Veith approach literary analysis from a Christian worldview perspective, while Adler and Van Doren wrote a comprehensive, classic guide to the art of reading. Each is an excellent resource for learning how to explore and appreciate literature.

Excellence in Literature: Reading and Writing through the Classics

Reading great literature takes much more than just skimming over the words on a page. It is a process that involves absorbing, understanding, and making decisions about what the author is communicating. Reading is active and can be as richly rewarding as you want it to be. Quick, fun reading can help to hone your basic reading skills, but you will need to add analysis in order to grow as a reader and writer. I hope you will enjoy the learning process.

Reading Challenging Literature

There is a general sequence that I have found helpful for reading the classics or any other challenging literature, and it is the sequence you will find in many of the EIL modules. If you need to use a different sequence, it will be noted in the week-by-week plan. Here is an overview:

- Read brief contextual information about the author and the historical time in which the book, poem, or play was written.

- If possible, listen to a bit of music that the author may have listened to, read at least one poem of the period, and look at an art history book or online to see what sort of art was being created at the time the book was written. This helps you gain an understanding of the author's artistic influences and can help you understand what you are reading.

- For the most challenging books, you may begin by reading a children's version or a brief synopsis of the work, such as those found in SparkNotes® or Cliff-Notes®. This is not necessary for most works, but I recommend it for those with archaic language, such as Chaucer's *Canterbury Tales* or for epic poetry such as Dante's *Inferno*. Although many people associate study guides with cheating, these guides are simply intended to help the student understand a work, just as a parent or teacher would do. Using them is cheating only if you read the guide, rather than the novel or poem. Once you have read the synopsis or children's version of a difficult book, you will be ready to read or listen to the complete text.

- Read the work all the way through, at a comfortable pace. Read fast enough to sustain interest, but slowly enough to understand what is happening. Focus on enjoying the story or poem.

- If the assignment is poetry or a play, listen to it (even if you have to read it aloud in order to do so) or watch it as suggested in the assignments. Poetry is meant to be heard, and plays are meant to be seen and heard, so you must do this in order to fully appreciate them.

- As you read, keep an index card or piece of paper tucked into the back of the book, or write on the blank end pages. Write down any words you do not know, look them up, and write down the definition. If you understand the basic meaning from the context, do not interrupt the flow of the story—just look up the word later.

- In your English notebook write down interesting insights that occur to you, as well as quotes that seem significant. Feel free to mark important or interesting passages in the book (I use a pencil, rather than a highlighter) so that you can easily find them to use as quotations while you are writing your essay.

- Once you have read the book, start the writing assignments. If you are working with a book not listed in this guide, write an approach paper according to the instructions in the Formats and Models chapter. The approach paper should include a brief summary, character analysis, discussion questions, key passage, and an explanation of the key passage. This will help you think through the book and prepare you for writing an essay.

- Write the assigned essay, answering the assigned essay prompt.

Reading Fiction

If you are reading fiction, you will need to notice how the five elements of **plot, theme, character, setting, and style** work together to create the alternate world of the story. However, while you are reading, it is also important to allow yourself to be immersed in the fictional world, to the point that when you stop reading, you feel as if you have just returned from a long journey. Immersion allows you to experience the author's creation as he or she intended. It also helps you to see the story as a whole when you begin to analyze the elements of the text.

As you read and try to understand, not just the surface meaning of the text but also the underlying theme and worldview, refer to the list of questions at the end of this chapter. Thinking about these can help you move deeper into the text.

As you look through the questions, you may find terms you do not know. Look them up in the Glossary of this guide, and if you need more information, consult your writer's handbook, or go to Google and type in "define:" (without the quotes) followed by the word or phrase you are looking for.

Reading Poetry

If you are reading poetry, there are a few other things to consider. Poetry uses structure, sound, and syntax to awaken the reader's imagination and to convey an image or message in a vivid and memorable way. A beautifully written poem can convey an idea in just a few unforgettable lines. If you have not studied the analysis of poetry, it is especially important to review the process in one or more of the resources I have recommended above, such as *How to Read Slowly* or your writer's handbook.

To begin understanding a poem, read it through slowly and carefully at least once or twice. Read it aloud, and listen to the sound of the words and pacing of the lines and syllables. Once you have the sound of the poem in your head, try paraphrasing it in prose. Think about each element and how the structure of the lines and the sound of the words contributes to the poem's theme. Examine the images, the rhyme scheme, and the sound patterns of the poem to help you understand the poet's message. Above all, read it through in its entirety often enough so that you see and remember it as a whole, just as you would look at a great painting as a whole before beginning to study the brush strokes.

Comedy and Tragedy

Although we sometimes think of comedy as something funny and tragedy as something sad, each word has a slightly different meaning in classic literature. Comedy is a story that begins with a conflict or suffering and ends in joy, such as *Jane Eyre* or *A Midsummer Night's Dream*.

Tragedy is a story that begins at a high point and ends in pain, such as *Romeo and Juliet* or *Oedipus Rex*. Aristotle further defined tragedy as the downfall of a noble human, in a disaster of his own making (*King Lear*). You will find a very enlightening chapter on comedy and tragedy in the Veith book, suggesting that in comedy can be seen an image of salvation, while in tragedy can be seen the shadow of damnation.

Facing Challenging Ideas

Great literature tends to mirror life. A book becomes a classic because it creates an honest and true picture of life and accurately depicts the consequences of various worldviews. In portraying life accurately, complex and sometimes unpleasant issues arise, just as they do in life. Characters do or say things that are deeply wrong, as Macbeth did in giving way to ambition and committing murder, or Peter Rabbit did in stealing carrots from Mr. MacGregor's garden. However, each character experienced appropriate, true-to-life consequences for his actions, which makes it possible for the reader to identify with and learn from the story.

Gene Edward Veith specifically cautions Christian readers not to "seize upon a detail [such as a "bad word"] or a subject dealt with by a book, take it completely out of context, and fail to do the necessary labor of thinking about the work and interpreting it thematically" (72) before they take a stand against the book. He also cautions against stories that do not tell the truth about life. "Stories filled with 'good people' overcoming all odds may create the dangerous impression that human beings are, in fact, 'good' and capable of saving themselves through their own moral actions" (76). This type of plot is often found in genre fiction—what I call "Twinkies® for the brain"—and is what keeps these books from being great literature even when they tell an enjoyable story.

Annotating

If you annotate your books as you read, you will understand and enjoy them more deeply than if you simply skim the text. Your annotations will also help you quickly locate important scenes in the book as you are doing the writing assignments for each module. Here are some suggestions for effective annotation.

Use a pencil for all writing in your books, as it does not show through and can be erased if necessary. Write on the inside of the covers or on the blank pages at the front and back of your focus text. Use an index card or piece of paper if you are using a library book.

- **Draw a vertical line** or star beside significant paragraphs you would like to remember.
- **Underline** important phrases or ideas.
- **Character List**: List each of the characters in the order in which they appear. Include a brief note about the character's role in the plot or any distinguishing characteristics.
- **Timeline**: List each major event in the story as it happens.
- **Context**: If the focus text mentions a person, a piece of art, literature, or music, or a historic event, make a note in the margin and look up the item. Many classical compositions can be found on YouTube.com. Just search by typing in the composer or composition name.
- **Questions**: If you have a question about something in the text, write it in the margin. Writing it down will help you recognize the answer if it later appears in the text. If it does not appear, the written question will remind you to do a bit more research.

Questions to Consider as You Read

If you are not familiar with the terms used in this list, look them up in the Glossary at the back of the guide or in your writer's handbook.

- Who is the **narrator** of the story, and is he or she reliable?

- What happens, and in what order does it happen (plot)?

- Can you identify the basic stages of the story structure—exposition (background information), rising action (complications), climax, falling action, resolution?

- How is the story told? Possibilities include first-person narrative, a journal, epistolary style (told as a series of letters), etc. How does this method affect your understanding of each of the story elements?

- Does the method of storytelling affect your enjoyment of the plot?

- Who are the major and minor characters, and what kind of people are they? Consider physical, mental, moral, and spiritual dimensions.

- Do the challenges of the main character reflect common struggles of humanity? Is the character intended to portray an archetype?

- What **symbolism** do you see, and how effectively does it enhance your understanding?

- What types of **conflict** do you see? Possibilities include man vs. man, man vs. God, man vs. nature, man vs. society, or even man vs. himself.

- What role does each character play in revealing the story?

- What **plot devices** does the author use to move the story along? Possibilities include flashbacks, narrative frames, foreshadowing, genre-specific conventions, and so forth.

- What are the **themes** or great ideas (justice, friendship, good vs. evil, etc.) addressed in this work? What theme is primary?

- How do the characters bring the theme to life?

- What is the author's vision of the meaning of life? Does he or she believe in the existence of good and evil? Of God? What is his or her view of humanity?

- Why has the author used a specific word rather than a synonym in the way and in the place he has used it? Would a synonym work as well? Why or why not?

How to Write an Essay

The time to begin writing an article is when you have finished it to your satisfaction. By that time you begin to clearly and logically perceive what it is you really want to say.

—Mark Twain

An essay is a short writing assignment on a particular subject. According to the *Oxford Shorter English Dictionary*, the word *essay* is derived from the Latin root *exigere*, which means to ascertain or weigh. It is also defined as "a first tentative attempt at learning, composition, etc.; a first draft." The essay is sometimes called a position paper, because it must be an expression of the writer's judgment, rather than a simple report.

Essays can be written to inform an audience, explain something, argue a position, or analyze an issue. Because the writer is expressing an opinion or interpretation, each essay can be seen as an attempt to persuade the reader that your thesis is plausible. Because the essay form involves all steps of the writing process, you will be able to apply the skills learned to any type of writing you do in the future.

In Excellence in Literature, you will have the opportunity to write essays, approach papers, literature summaries, and author profiles. The essay prompt in each module will provide an exact subject, and you will find that writing itself will turn into a process of discovery. You will rarely know the answer to the questions in the essay prompt until you begin writing, but as you begin to formulate a thesis and write analytically, you will begin to understand the subject at a much deeper level than if you had simply read the book.

The Writing Process

The three canons of classical composition are Invention, Arrangement, and Elocution.

- Invention, also called Discovery, is the process of coming up with ideas;
- Arrangement, otherwise known as Disposition, is the process of placing ideas in logical order;
- Elocution, sometimes referred to as Style, is the process of appropriately expressing ideas.

Essentially, every writer must gather ideas, put them in order, and write them in a way that is understandable and appealing. To do this, I recommend the following writing process:

1. Invention
   - Read/Research
   - Think on Paper
2. Arrangement
   - Organize Ideas
3. Elocution
   - Write
   - Revise

Read and Research

To begin an essay assignment, gather information through reading and research. For Excellence in Literature assignments, this means you will read the focus text and assigned context resources, plus any other resources that seem relevant. Be sure to choose research materials from reliable sources such as published encyclopedias and reference books, college websites, and original source documents.

Think on Paper with a Mind Map

To Think on Paper, the second step of the writing process, you will begin to connect reading and research with the essay prompt. I use the process of mind mapping as a tool for thinking on paper. This allows ideas and supporting points to be quickly recorded in an organic form that encourages the flow of ideas. Here is an example of a simple mind map.

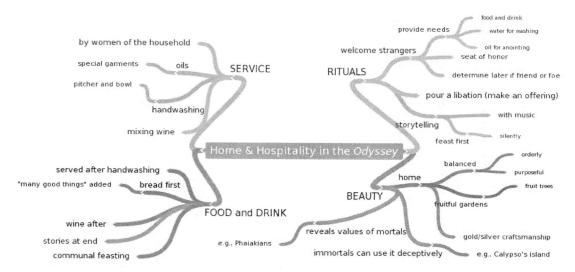

How to Think on Paper

- At the center of your paper, write a few words that summarize the topic or question you are supposed to answer.

- Draw a line radiating from the center idea for each relevant fact, possible argument, proof point, or supporting detail that comes to mind.

- Branch off these ideas as additional details emerge.

- Write down everything that comes to mind, even if you are not sure it fits. Generating ideas is like turning on a faucet for hot water. What comes out at first is not hot, but it has to come out before what you really want can emerge. Your best ideas usually begin to flow after your mind has warmed up and settled into thinking about a topic.

- Record each idea on the mind map as a word or phrase rather than a complete sentence, and feel free to use symbols and abbreviations to briefly capture your idea.

Additional Mind Mapping Ideas

- You may use color in your mind maps, but it is best not to create an elaborate color coding scheme, as this can impede the flow of ideas.

- Some people prefer to use quick sketches rather than words to capture some or all of their ideas. If this is the way your mind works, and it does not slow you down too much, you may do this.

- Mind maps are usually made with pen or pencil on paper, but the sample above was created with a free web app called Coggle.it. Do what works for you.

- You can see many examples of mind maps at http://www.tonybuzan.com/gallery/mind-maps/

Organize Ideas

Once you have generated several ideas, you must decide which ideas best fit the essay assignment, and how they might logically flow. Begin by dividing ideas into three categories: Affirmative, Negative, and Interesting (sometimes known as Pro, Con, and Interesting). Once you have categorized ideas, you will probably have more than you need, so select the most compelling points, and either number them on your mind map, or list them in a logical sequence.

Look at the ordered ideas, and determine whether your thesis will be an Affirmative or Negative answer to the essay prompt, or whether you will take an equivocal position in which you provide evidence for and against both sides of the question.

Thesis Statement

Draft a thesis statement that outlines your position and describes how you will support your argument. In its most elementary form, the thesis can be as simple as a transformation of the essay prompt into a thesis statement. Here is an example of what this looks like:

Question (adapted from a portion of the essay prompt in *American Literature* Module 2):

- How did the courtship strategies of Irving's characters compare to those of Longfellow's characters?

Question transformed into a thesis statement:

- Although Bram Bones and John Alden were successful in their respective courtships, their courtship strategies differed from one another in several specific ways, including [insert three ways here].

The thesis statement would usually appear near the end of the introductory paragraph, completing the job of orienting the reader to the topic and your position.

Topic Sentence Outline

Transform your list of supporting points into an essay framework by writing a topic sentence (TS) outline. Topic sentences introduce each supporting paragraph in the body of the essay and announce the proof you will be presenting in that paragraph.

Following the topic sentence will be two or more sentences supporting the argument or providing the information found in the topic sentence. Here is an example of a topic sentence outline:

Sample Outline For a Short Essay on Homer[2]

General Subject: Homer's *Odyssey*

Focus 1: The importance of the home and hospitality

Focus 2: Home and hospitality in *The Odyssey*: the significance of food

Thesis: In *The Odyssey*, the frequent and detailed attention to food and the rituals surrounding it serve constantly to reinforce a central concern of the poem, the vital civilizing importance of the home.

TS 1: Throughout *The Odyssey*, we witness the way in which food taken communally can act as a way of reenergizing human beings, enabling them to cope with their distress. This, in fact, emerges as one of the most important human values in the poem. (Paragraph argues for the restorative values of food as brought out repeatedly in the poem.)

TS 2: The rituals surrounding food, especially the importance of welcoming guests to the feast and making sure everyone has enough, stress the warmth and central importance of open human interaction. (The paragraph argues the importance of hospitality as it is brought out by the references to food and feasting.)

TS 3: The occasions in which food is consumed are also moments in which the participants celebrate the artistic richness of their culture. No where else in the poem is there so much attention paid to the significance of beauty in various forms.

---

[2]This sample excerpted from the *Excellence in Literature Handbook for Writers* by Ian Johnston and Janice Campbell.

(Paragraph X argues that all the things associated with the food—the serving dishes, the entertainment, and so on—reflect important values in the culture.)

Conclusion: There is, of course, much more to the poem than the description of feasting, but we need to recognize these moments as especially important. (Paragraph restates and summarizes the central point of the argument.)

Note: Remain flexible as you write, because it is quite possible to discover another angle or better idea as you are writing. If this happens, do not worry about sticking exactly to your outline. The outline is simply a tool for organization, so you, as the author, are still in charge. Do what works.

Write the Essay

Once you have organized your ideas into an outline, it is time to begin writing. At this stage, you have thoroughly thought through the question and your ideas, and have a sturdy framework to build on. Begin writing your first draft, following the outline you have created.

Type your paper on the computer, following the formatting instructions contained in "Making Your Essay Look Good: The Basics of MLA Format," the last example in the Formats and Models chapter. At this stage, your primary concerns will be to successfully answer the essay prompt and to support your argument with relevant examples from the text. Look at the rubric in the back of the book to remind yourself of standards goals in the content, style, and mechanics of the paper.

Revise

When the draft is completed, read it aloud to yourself. This will help you pinpoint areas that seem unclear or poorly expressed. Do not skip this step! As you find things that need to be fixed, mark them and keep reading, so you do not lose the flow of the text. When you are finished, go through and fix the things you have marked. When it is as good as you can make it, turn it in.

When you receive the paper back from your writing mentor, read it aloud once again. You may be surprised to notice additional ways in which you can improve it. Refer to the evaluation rubric that you receive along with the essay, and make any improvements recommended there or in your teacher's marginal comments. Focus on fine tuning the style of the paper, including word choice, sentence fluency, and voice. You will find basic standards for these areas listed on the rubric, but your writer's handbook will help you learn even more.

Finally, when you have completed the edits recommended by your teacher, and you feel your essay meets the standards listed on the rubric, read it aloud once more. Change anything that does not sound right, check the mechanics, and when you are satisfied, turn it in.

As you follow this simple, orderly process in assignment after assignment, it will become automatic for you, and writing will become easier. By the time you reach college, you will be able to confidently tackle any writing assignment you encounter. I wish you joy in the rigorous study of the craft of writing.

Resources You May Find Helpful

The Elegant Essay Writing Lessons by Lesha Myers

Excellence in Literature Handbook for Writers

The Lost Tools of Writing from the Circe Institute

The Mind Map Book by Tony Buzan

Teaching Writing: Structure and Style from Institute for Excellence in Writing

Writing to Learn by WIlliam Zinsser

Discerning Worldview through
Literary Periods

Do you ever wonder why it is that many of history's titanic intellects managed to come to radically different conclusions? The answer is simple: If you begin your system of thought by refusing to acknowledge what you know to be true—if you start with a lie—the more brilliant and consistent you are in following that premise, the further from truth you will go.

—Tim Challies

When you are studying literature in context, literary periods can help you understand the ideas of the underlying worldview of each era. Each literary period is characterized by specific philosophical movements and historical events that affected the art, literature, and music of the day. If you have a good grasp of the assumptions that shaped each period, you will understand something of the author's worldview before you even read the book.

There are six major periods or movements in English language literature, and each is described below with its approximate time frame. Each period has sub-periods within it, as well as overlapping characteristics. I have chosen to adapt and use the system of categories used by Adam Andrews in *Teaching the Classics with Worldview Supplement*, as I think it is an excellent, simple introduction to the subject. The literary period descriptions have been adapted, with permission, from the *Worldview Supplement.*

Medieval (AD 500–1500)	Renaissance (1500–1660)
Neoclassical (1660–1800)	Romantic (1800–1865)
Realist (1840–1914)	Modernist (1900–1945)

Medieval (AD 500–1500)

The **Medieval** period includes the Anglo-Saxon period in the time before the 1066 Norman conquest of England, and the Middle English period after the conquest. Anglo-Saxon literature, which is based on oral storytelling, focuses on the heroic ideal which involved responsibility, leadership, loyalty, generosity, and skill in battle. After Christianity reached Britain in the seventh century, literature became overwhelmingly Christian in its themes, while still retaining its concern for the heroic ideal. The epic poem *Beowulf* is a characteristic work from this period.

The **Middle English** period was marked by a change in the purpose and audience for written literature. Anglo-Saxon works had been written by and for the aristocracy, but Middle English literature was by and for people of the lower classes. Rather than the idealized king-heros of the Anglo-Saxon period, Middle English heros were everyday people living in everyday situations. Christianity remained central to the medieval world, and most literature reflected this priority. This literary movement roughly coincided with the Gothic period in art and architecture. The best-known work of this period is *The Canterbury Tales* by Geoffrey Chaucer.

Renaissance (1500–1660)

The Renaissance period was a flamboyant, fervent era of exploration and expansion, characterized by several movements, including Renaissance humanism, the Protestant Reformation, and English Nationalism. Renaissance writers were concerned with classical learning, the study of the humanities (language, literature, history, art, and government), the function of true religion in the world, and interest in the form and structure of human government. This literary movement roughly coincided with the baroque period in art, music, and architecture.

Authors you will recognize from this period include William Shakespeare, Edmund Spenser, John Donne, and Anne Bradstreet.

Neoclassical (1660–1800)

The Neoclassical period in literature, art, and music roughly coincided with the Age of Enlightenment. Writers in the Neoclassical period favored simplicity, clarity, restraint, regularity, and good sense, as opposed to the intricacy and boldness of the Renaissance period. Neoclassical writers sought to discover meaning in the order of things, placed society before the individual, and valued human reason over natural passions. Many of these writers were influenced by the rise of experimental science and the desire for peace and stability. Many sought to imitate the style of Roman writers such as Virgil and Ovid. The art and music of this period reflected the aesthetic values of this literary movement.

Writers of this period include Benjamin Franklin, Daniel Defoe, and Jonathan Swift.

Romantic (1800–1865)

Following the French Revolution there was general movement away from the formal literature of the Neoclassical period. Romantic art, music, and literature reflected a belief in mankind's innate goodness, equality, and potential for achievement, and strongly rejected the Neoclassical view of man as a limited being in a strictly hierarchical society. Possibly as a reaction against urbanization and other challenges of the Industrial Revolution, nature was prominently featured as a symbol of freedom of the human soul, and scenic beauty as a model for harmony. Emotion, imagination, and intuition were valued above reason and restraint. This period includes Early and Mid-Victorian literature.

Authors in this tradition include Jane Austen, Sir Walter Scott, James Fenimore Cooper, and Henry David Thoreau.

Realist (1840–1914)

Just as Romantic writers had rejected Neoclassical ideas, Realist authors, artists, and musicians rejected Romantic notions. Realists sought to portray the world and man without idealism, so their works dealt with issues such as industrialization, poverty, and inequality, sometimes focusing on the ugly or sordid. They were interested in the relationship between traditional religion, rationalist thought, and new philosophies such as Darwinism. In England, the Realist period takes place largely during the reign of Queen Victoria (1837–1901), so it includes Mid- and Late Victorian literature.

Realist writers you may know include Charles Dickens, the Brontë sisters, and Mark Twain.

One form of realism that lasted until World War II was known as **Naturalism**. Influenced by Charles Darwin's theory of evolution, Naturalist writers believed that social conditions, heredity, and environment, rather than Providence or Fate, determined man's destiny, and they often wrote about those on the fringe of society, including the uncouth and sordid. If Romantics saw the individual as a god and Realists saw him as a common man, Naturalists saw him as a helpless animal for whom free will was only an illusion.

Naturalist writers include Jack London and Stephen Crane. Edith Wharton is sometimes included in this list as well.

Modernist (1900–1945)

The dramatic changes wrought by the Industrial Revolution, Marxism, and modern scientific theories and political developments rocked the faith of twentieth-century writers. At the heart of Modernist literature is a reflection of their conviction that all the traditional structures of human life—religious, social, political, economic, and artistic—had either been destroyed or proven false. The writers' disorientation and uncertainty is often seen in the fragmented form of their fiction, and their protagonists are often aimless and frustrated rather than heroic.

Modernist authors include F. Scott Fitzgerald, Gertrude Stein, T.S. Eliot, Ernest Hemingway, Ezra Pound, and Willa Cather.

After World War II, the Modernist movement split into fragments such as Post-Modernism, Imagism, the Harlem Renaissance, Surrealism, Beat poets, Post-colonialists, and others. It is not clear which, if any, of these will prove dominant in historic hindsight. What is certain is that each of the literary periods explored here will help you understand the literature you read, in the context in which it was created.

This summary of literary periods is adapted from Teaching the Classics, *and is used courtesy of Adam Andrews. For an introduction to literary analysis and additional description of the literary periods, please see* Teaching the Classics with Worldview Supplement *by Adam and Missy Andrews of The Center for Literary Education at www.CenterForLit.com.*

Using EIL in a Classroom

I have been hearing of many ways teachers are using this curriculum in classrooms and co-ops. Eventually, I hope to establish a spot on Excellence-in-Literature.com for teachers to exchange ideas and find support, but until then, here are few suggestions.

First, remember that one of the key features of EIL is the practice of college-level learning skills in addition to literary analysis. This means that students should be heavily involved in context research and discussions about the text. The teacher or co-op leader should be functioning in the role of a facilitator, assigning areas of research and guiding discussions, rather than doing the research and lecturing on findings.

As Charlotte Mason admonished, "We err when we allow our admirable teaching to intervene between children and the knowledge their minds demand. The desire for knowledge (curiosity) is the chief agent in education: but this desire may be made powerless like an unused limb" (*A Philosophy of Education*, p. 247). She asks, "What if the devitalisation we notice in so many of our young people, keen about games but dead to things of the mind, is due to the processes carried on in our schools, to our plausible and pleasant ways of picturing, eliciting, demonstrating, illustrating, summarising, doing all those things for children which they are born with the potency to do for themselves?" (p. 237). Simply stated, learning happens when students interact with literature, not when they listen passively to a lecture.

Here are a few ideas for creating an active group learning environment:

- Introduce each module by pointing the student to the Module Focus, Literary Context, and Introduction in the text.

- Assign a context area to each student or group of students, and have them report their findings to the class.

- If the Focus Text is a poem, encourage students to listen to at least a portion of it in a professionally recorded audio version. A poem is meant to be heard, and listening will bring it to life as nothing else can.

- For each module, have students choose one passage or poem to recite or copy by hand. Recitation and copywork both aid retention of ideas and build writing skills, as both require close attention to the use of words and sequence of ideas.

- If the Focus Text is a play, always try to watch the video version. It may be best to watch it after the focus text has been read, so students will be able to appreciate subtle twists and nuances they may otherwise miss.

- Use the *Something to Think About* and *Be Sure to Notice* items as discussion starters after students have begun reading the text.

- Encourage additional research or sharing of context items not found in the EIL guide. If students find a resource they particularly like, they are welcome to submit it to me at janice@eilit.com for possible inclusion in the next edition of EIL.

- When students do an approach paper, choose some of their discussion questions to spark discussions in class. If students have chosen different key passages (this is perfectly fine), encourage them to discuss why they chose the passage they did, and why it is key.

- When students have finished the focus text, encourage discussion of how it exemplifies its literary period, and ways it may have differed from student expectations.

- If you choose to watch the movie version of a novel as part of the class, discuss how it differs from the author's creation.

- Encourage comparison of the current focus text with other works the student has read in or out of class. As they learn to discern common themes, you may find them referencing *Les Misérables*, *Merchant of Venice*, *The Little Red Hen*, and *The Lion, the Witch and the Wardrobe* in a discussion of justice and mercy. This means they are seeing through each story into the broader story beyond, and that is what it means to read with understanding.

- If you have five classroom periods each week, use one to practice what my high school used to call USSR—Uninterrupted, Sustained, Silent Reading. Many students have never been required to sit quietly for an hour and do anything, but this is an essential skill that needs to be learned, and USSR is a good way to begin. (For more on brain development and the effect of technology on language skills, I recommend *Endangered Minds* and *Failure to Connect* by Dr. Jane Healy.)

Comprehension Questions

I do not believe in using "comprehension questions" at all, except in a limited way as practice for necessary standardized testing. I do not believe they are useful or effective, especially for high school students who should be learning to think critically and write analytically about the literature they read.

Comprehension questions are usually trivia questions which test only student memory or the ability to catch details. Instead of helping students think deeply about the text as a whole, comprehension questions often make reading nothing more than a treasure hunt for answers. I have seen "how to study" guides that suggest students should read the comprehension questions first, then hunt for answers as they skim the story. This may be an effective strategy for timed standardized tests and may seem to be a quick and easy way to finish an assignment and move on, but it completely short circuits the learning process.

The writing prompts provided in EIL encourage students to think critically and analyze something specific about the text. It is impossible to write a coherent, thoughtful paper without comprehending the text, so it provides a much better measure of how much the student understands about the literary work, and how well he or she writes.

Quick Guide to Excellence in Literature Learning Tools

This handy chart will help you remember some EIL basics.

Writing Process
1. Read/Research
2. Think on Paper
3. Organize
4. Write
5. Revise

p. 35

Basic Literary Periods
• Medieval
• Renaissance
• Neoclassical
• Romantic
• Realist
• Modernist

p. 41

Pencil Annotations
• Draw vertical line beside important paragraphs.
• Underline important ideas or themes.

Inside Covers
• List characters in order of appearance.
• Make a timeline of events in the story.
• Note context items to look up.

p. 28

Evaluation Criteria
• **Content**
  · ideas/concepts
  · organization
• **Style**
  · voice
  · sentence fluency
  · word choice
• Mechanics
  · conventions
  · presentation

p. 138

Formats and Models
• Approach Paper Model
• Historic/Event Approach Paper Model
• Author Profile Model
• Literature Summary Model
• Literary Analysis Model
• Poetry Analysis Model
• MLA Format Model Model

p. 121

MLA Page Setup
• 1" margins
• Times New Roman or similar font
• 12 point font size

p. 135

Tip: Remember to space once, not twice, after terminal punctuation (periods, question marks, etc.).

Learning Cycle
Weeks 1 & 2
• Read text and context resources.
• Do a short assignment each week.

Week 3
• Write essay or creative assignment.
• Turn in for evaluation of content and organization.

Week 4
• Revise assignment according to evaluation feedback.
• Turn in for evaluation of all standards on rubric.

Word Count Equivalent
• 250 words = one double-sided page typed in MLA format

Honors Texts
• Short Stories
• *20,000 Leagues Under the Sea* by Verne
• *The Prince and the Pauper* by Twain
• *Villette* or *Shirley* by Brontë
• *Murder in the Cathedral* by Eliot
• *Kidnapped* by Stevenson
• *1984* by Orwell *Fahrenheit 461* by Bradbury
• *A Midsummer Night's Dream* by Shakespeare
• *Pilgrim's Progress* by Bunyan

What to do for the optional Honors Track:

• Read honors texts.
• Do approach paper on one honors text.
• Write research paper.
• Take CLEP test (optional).

p. 116

Prerequisites for Success
• Have grade-level skills in language arts.

Commitment to
• read instructions;
• refer to a writer's handbook as needed;
• revise according to feedback.

p. 9

Focus Texts
• *Robinson Crusoe* by DeFoe
• *Around the World in Eighty Days* by Verne
• *A Connecticut Yankee in King Arthur's Court* by Twain
• *Jane Eyre* by Brontë
• *Pygmalion* by Shaw
• *Treasure Island* by Stevenson
• *Animal Farm* by Orwell
• *The Tempest* by Shakespeare
• *Gulliver's Travels* by Swift

Necessary Resources
• writer's handbook

Optional Resources
• dictionary
• thesaurus
• calendar for scheduling
• English notebook to store your papers

p. 18

Remember
• Follow weekly schedule for each module.
• Use the Formats and Models as a guide.
• If you have questions about grammar, style, or mechanics, consult your writer's handbook.

Websites to Remember
• Context Resources: www.Excellence-in-Literature.com
• Writing Reference at Purdue Online Lab: owl.english.purdue.edu/owl/

Module 2.1

Robinson Crusoe by Daniel DeFoe (c. 1660–1731)

Thus we never see the true State of our Condition, till it is illustrated to us by its Contraries; nor know how to value what we enjoy, but by the want of it..

—Robinson Crusoe

Focus Text

Robinson Crusoe by Daniel DeFoe

Honors Texts

The Swiss Family Robinson by Johann David Wyss and/or

The Further Adventures of Robinson Crusoe by Daniel DeFoe

Literary Period

Neoclassical

Module Focus

You will become familiar with the conventions of spiritual autobiography (a story that begins with a sinful youth, spiritual awakening, anxiety about the soul's future, repentance, an attempt at living a good life, backsliding, further repentance, and a final epiphany that results in true salvation and peace with God) and the way that real events can help to shape a novel.

Introduction

Robinson Crusoe is one of the earliest and most widely known English novels. With its absorbing tale of the survivial of a lone castaway, it has captured the imagination of both children and adults. Its author, Daniel DeFoe, was a Presbyterian dissenter, and his political and religious beliefs can be discerned throughout the story, as can elements of his life as a merchant. As you read the story, enjoy the adventure, but be sure to notice what DeFoe seems to be saying about God, religion, man versus nature, capitalism, and the social values of his day.

Something to think about . . .

The 1719 edition of *Robinson Crusoe* sported an impressive title: *The Life and Strange Surprizing Adventures of Robinson Crusoe, of York, Mariner: Who lived Eight and Twenty Years, all alone in an uninhabited Island on the Coast of America, near the Mouth of the Great River of Oroonoque; Having been cast on Shore by Shipwreck, wherein all the Men perished but himself. With An Account how he was at last as strangely deliver'd by Pyrates.* What do you think was the purpose of this title? Does it make you more or less interested in reading the story?

Be sure to notice . . .

During the 17th century, spiritual autobiography was a very popular form of writing that described the writer's journey from sin, through repentance, and into salvation. Although it is a work of fiction, there are ways in which *Robinson Crusoe* maintains the conventions of the spiritual autobiography. Be sure to notice this as you read or listen through the book.

Context Resources

Alexander Selkirk is the Scottish seaman whose true story apparently inspired Daniel DeFoe to write *Robinson Crusoe*. Read about his adventures and consider how his story compares with that of the fictional Crusoe.

http://www.nationalarchives.gov.uk/pathways/blackhistory/journeys/voyage_html/selkirk.htm

http://www.smithsonianmag.com/history-archaeology/crusoe.html

Christian History Timeline offers a brief look at the relationship of Alexander Selkirk's story to *Robinson Crusoe*. DeFoe may have been inspired by other influences, but Selkirk is the most widely known.

http://www.christianhistorytimeline.com/DAILYF/2002/02/daily-02-02-2002.shtml

A professor at Brooklyn College has posted a very helpful study guide on "Religion in *Robinson Crusoe*." Print this out and refer to it as you read through the book. Be sure to notice the chart on Puritan symbolism, and to think about whether you agree with the author's perspective on DeFoe's justification of providence. (There is not a "right" answer to this question; rather, it is a matter of whether DeFoe was able to justify providence to your satisfaction. Every reader must decide this for himself, and the decision will be largely based on the reader's worldview and background, and supported with quotes from the text. Reasonable people will differ, and that is okay—that is why literary analysis is fun and interesting.)

http://excellence-in-literature.com/excellence-in-lit/intro-to-lit/e1-resources/religion-in-robinson-crusoe-by-lilia-melani

If you have the *Norton Anthology of English Literature,* read the section on "Trade, Travel, and the Expansion of Empire" in the "The Restoration and the Eighteenth Century" chapter. If you do not have the book, there is a brief overview online.

http://www.wwnorton.com/college/english/nael/18century/topic_4/welcome.htm

The Author's Life

If your library has a good middle-grade biography of Daniel DeFoe, read it. Otherwise, read about Daniel DeFoe in your encyclopedia or online:

http://www.britannica.com/EBchecked/topic/155842/Daniel-Defoe

http://www.notablebiographies.com/De-Du/Defoe-Daniel.html

Poetry

John Dryden is a Neoclassical poet described as "the author in whose work the image of an age can be discerned" (*Norton Anthology of English Literature*, Vol. 1., 1786).

Much of his poetry is political or religious in nature. Read these two poems in your anthology or at the link below.

- "Veni, Creator Spiritus"
- "Alexander's Feast"

http://excellence-in-literature.com/lit-and-comp/e2-resources/john-dryden-poetry

"The Tree" by Anne Finch, Countess of Winchilsea (1661-1720) is another poem in the Neoclassical tradition. The poet William Wordsworth enjoyed Finch's work.

http://excellence-in-literature.com/lit-and-comp/e2-resources/the-tree-by-anne-finch

English poet Gerard Manley Hopkins (1844-1889) tells the story of "The Wreck of the Deutschland (Dec. 6, 7, 1875)." This is a challenging poem, so you do not have to read the entire thing. Notice how Hopkins' unique poetic style differs from the Neoclassical works you have read.

Background information about Hopkins and the Deutschland:

http://www.poets.org/poet.php/prmPID/284

The poem:

http://excellence-in-literature.com/lit-and-comp/e2-resources/
the-wreck-of-the-deutschland-by-gerard-manley-hopkins

Be sure to also read "God's Grandeur," one of Hopkins' most beautiful works. In order to fully appreciate Hopkins' creative style, I recommend copying (by hand) one of his poems in your notebook.

http://excellence-in-literature.com/british-lit/e4-resources/
gods-grandeur-by-gerard-manley-hopkins

Richard Austin is an actor who specializes in reciting Hopkins' poetry from memory. If you ever have an opportunity to attend one of his live performances, do not miss it! Listening to Mr. Austin bring Hopkins' poetry to life is an unforgettable experience.

http://www.richard.austin.sh

Audio

If you enjoy listening to books, your library may have *Robinson Crusoe* on CD. If not, you can find a free amateur recording of the novel on Librivox.

http://librivox.org/robinson-crusoe-by-daniel-defoe/

Video

Chasing Crusoe is an outstanding multimedia project developed by a university class. It offers a look at the parallels between Crusoe and Selkirk as well as pirates, privateers, and sailing ships. Do not miss it!

http://www.rcrusoe.org/home_eng.html

There have been several movies and a television show made of *Robinson Crusoe* in the last fifty years or so, but I have not seen them. If you would like to watch one, I recommend reading reviews in a reliable movie guide.

There is a 1927 silent film of *Robinson Crusoe* that is available online:

http://excellence-in-literature.com/lit-and-comp/e2-resources/
robinson-crusoe-1927-silent-film

Visual Arts

Artist N.C. Wyeth painted evocative illustrations for *Robinson Crusoe*. You can see them in the abridged version (by Timothy Meis) or online.

http://wyeth.artpassions.net/

"The Shipwreck" by Claude Joseph Vernet is the focus of a nicely done virtual tour from the National Gallery of Art. Follow the arrows through the tour, reading about the details of the painting, the artist's life, and about other seascapes, including a comparison of "Estuary at Dawn" by Simon de Vlieger with "The Shipwreck."

http://www.nga.gov/feature/artnation/vernet/index.shtm

Music

Jacques Offenbach wrote an opéra comique called *Robinson Crusoé* which was first performed at the Opéra-Comique in Paris in 1867. You may listen to a few minutes of it in this YouTube video:

http://excellence-in-literature.com/excellence-in-lit/lit-and-comp/e2-resources/opera-robinson-crusoe

You may hear a little of the theme music from the 1970's television show of *Robinson Crusoe*.

http://excellence-in-literature.com/excellence-in-lit/lit-and-comp/e2-resources/soundtrack-1970s-for-robinson-crusoe-television-show

Historic Context

For context, read about shipwrecks and cannibalism in your encyclopedia.

Eyewitness Pirate by Richard Platt from Dorling Kindersley: Crusoe was captured by pirates. Look at this book to learn a little more about pirates and what they do.

On this fan site, inspired by the original three-volume edition of *Robinson Crusoe*, you will find a map and photo tour of the island of Tobago, with details about why the site's author believes this to be the inspiration for Crusoe's island.

http://www.robinsoncrusoe.ca/photovisit.htm

Just For Fun

Here is an amusing consideration of the improbabilities in *Robinson Crusoe* from an old book called *Handy-book of Literary Curiosities* by William Shepard Walsh.

"It has been said that everything in *Robinson Crusoe* might be demonstrated mathematically, that the writer, as with the instincts of a Scott or a Shakespeare, had got inside the shipwrecked mariner's mind. Yet even Defoe had his idiotic area. How, for example, did Crusoe manage to stuff his pockets with biscuits, when he had taken off all his clothes before swimming to the wreck? And when the clothes he had taken off were washed away by the tide, why did he not remember that he had all the ship's stores to choose from? How could he have seen the goat's eyes in the cave, when it was pitch dark ? How could the Spaniards have given Friday's father an agreement in writing, when they had neither paper nor ink? And, finally, how could Friday be so intimately acquainted with the habits of the bear, when that animal is not a denizen of the West Indian islands?

The imitators of *Robinson Crusoe* were even worse. Those readers who can cast back their minds to the days when they read *The Swiss Family Robinson* will recollect the extraordinary fecundity and native wealth of the island in which those lucky waifs resided. Not a fruit but flourished, not an edible bird or beast but inhabited that astounding latitude, and what was even more wonderful than the abundance of incongruous and incompatible forms of natural wealth was the success of every enterprise which any member of the family undertook."

If you are working on this unit in a co-op or class setting, you may enjoy this interesting group activity related to "Island Survival."

http://www.sitesalive.com/il/tg/private/iltgsurvival.htm

Read Beatrix Potter's *Tale of Little Pig Robinson*. Notice that it draws from both "The Owl and the Pussycat" by Edward Lear and from *Robinson Crusoe*.

Tale of Little Pig Robinson

http://www.childrensbooksonline.org/Tale_of_Little_Pig_Robinson/index.htm

"The Owl and the Pussy-Cat"

http://excellence-in-literature.com/lit-and-comp/e2-resources/
the-owl-and-the-pussy-cat-by-edward-lear

Assignment Schedule

Week 1

Read and explore context materials, and begin reading focus text. Follow the model in the Formats and Models chapter to write an Author Profile. Be sure to refer to your writer's handbook if you have questions about grammar, structure, or style.

Week 2

Writing in the style of a magazine article, advise readers of ways to survive if they are shipwrecked on a deserted island. Use examples from your reading to support your advice, and create a list of recommended supplies. This should be at least 300 words.

Alternate Assignment

Consider what would happen if you were stranded on a deserted island. Would the technology of today give you an advantage over Crusoe? If you could choose only seven items to help you survive, what would they be? If you could choose seven books you'd most like to be stranded with, what are they, and why would you choose each of them? Describe your survival items and books in 300 or more words.

In addition to the context links in this module, you may use other resources such as your encyclopedia, the library, and quality Internet resources to complete this assignment.

Week 3

Begin drafting a 500-word paper on one of the topics below. I recommend that you follow the writing process outlined in the "How to Write an Essay" chapter, consulting the models in the Formats and Models chapter and your writer's handbook as needed. 3

1- Model: Literary Analysis Essay and MLA Format Model

Prompt: Crusoe devotes many of the early years on the island to trying to find a way of escape from it. At the end of the book, however, after he is rescued and returns to England, he finds himself dreaming of returning to the island (and if you read *The Further Adventures of Robinson Crusoe*, you will find that he does return). What has changed to make this possible—Crusoe, the island, England, or all of them? Explain the changes that have taken place, and why they may have made Crusoe long for his island. Support your ideas with examples and quotes from the text.

Week 4

Use the feedback on the rubric, along with the writing mentor's comments, to revise your paper. Before turning in the final draft, be sure you have addressed any issues marked on the evaluation rubric, and verify that the thesis is clear and your essay is well-organized. Use your writer's handbook to check grammar or punctuation so that your essay will be free from mechanical errors. Turn in the essay at the end of the week so that the writing mentor can use the evaluation rubric in the "How to Evaluate" chapter to check your work.

Module 2.2

Walden by Henry David Thoreau (1817–1862)

*If a man does not keep pace with his companions, perhaps it is because he hears a different drummer.
Let him step to the music which he hears, however measured or far away.*

—Henry David Thoreau

Focus Text

Walden by Henry David Thoreau

Honors Text

"Civil Disobedience" by Henry David Thoreau and

"Self-Reliance" by Ralph Waldo Emerson

Literary Period

American Romanticism

Module Focus

As you study *Walden*, you will learn about the Transcendentalist movement, and observe the characteristics of Romanticism in Thoreau's memoir.

Introduction

Walden is Henry David Thoreau's memoir of a two-year period in which he lived alone in the woods near Walden Pond in Massachusetts. He writes about his purpose in living there, and makes many observations about life and society. His work has endured not only because of his interesting ideas, but also because he writes beautiful, vivid prose.

Something to think about . . .

Thoreau's idea was to live in the woods for a time "because I wished to live deliberately, to front only the essential facts of life, and see if I could not learn what it had to teach, and not, when I came to die, discover that I had not lived." As you are reading *Walden*, try to discern what he believes to be the "essential facts of life." Do you agree or disagree with his conclusions?

Be sure to notice . . .

Thoreau uses a variety of literary techniques in his prose. How do techniques such as metaphor and paradox help Thoreau establish a mood and convey his message?

Context Resources

Readings

The Thoreau Society has provided complete annotated versions of Thoreau's works online, along with a number of useful essays and links:

http://thoreau.eserver.org/default.html

Print out this timeline of Concord, Massachusetts from 1800-1890. You'll find it interesting and helpful to see how Thoreau's life intersected the lives of other writers in the area. Just imagine living around all that creativity!

http://www.wsu.edu/~campbelld/amlit/concord.htm

This excellent overview of Romanticism from Dr. Paul Brians (Washington State University) will help you understand the Romantic worldview, and in particular, its European roots.

http://public.wsu.edu/~brians/hum_303/romanticism.html

Read about the distinguishing characteristics of American Romanticism in this introduction to the period, by Dr. Ann Woodlief of VCU.

http://excellence-in-literature.com/lit-and-comp/e2-resources/
introduction-to-american-romanticism-by-ann-woodlief

The PBS-sponsored site, "I Hear America Singing," features good profiles of Thoreau, Louisa May and Bronson Alcott, and Ralph Waldo Emerson.

Thoreau: http://www.pbs.org/wnet/ihas/poet/thoreau.html

Alcotts: http://www.pbs.org/wnet/ihas/poet/alcotts.html

Emerson: http://www.pbs.org/wnet/ihas/poet/emerson.html

English teacher Ken Kifer has created a brief analytical overview of the contents of each chapter of *Walden*. Quite helpful.

http://www.phred.org/~alex/kenkifer/www.kenkifer.com/thoreau/index.htm

If you have not read *Little Women* by Louisa May Alcott, do so. This is fiction, but is based upon the author's life. Because the Alcotts were friends of Thoreau, this book will give you another window into Thoreau's time and place in history.

The Author's Life

Read a brief biography from your encyclopedia or the library. The *Cambridge History of English and American Literature* offers an authoritative overview of Thoreau's life and works in eleven brief segments. Read through them in order.

http://www.bartleby.com/226/

The Wilderness Stewardship site offers a brief biography of Thoreau.

http://www.wilderness.net/index.cfm?fuse=feature1208

Here are three views of Thoreau from other writers of the time—Ralph Waldo Emerson, Robert Louis Stevenson, and John Burroughs. Be sure to read the final entry—the "Pity and Humor" letter that directly addresses Stevenson's article (it is also listed specifically as the second link below).

http://thoreau.eserver.org/hdtx3.html

http://thoreau.eserver.org/japp.html

Do you know how Thoreau is connected to the lead pencil? Find out in this *Concord Magazine* article.

http://www.concordma.com/magazine/nov98/pencil.html

Poetry

This page offers a selection of poems, each of which is related to Thoreau in some way. It includes a memorial poem by Louisa May Alcott.

http://thoreau.eserver.org/poetry.html#encountr

Audio

Librivox offers a free, amateur recording of *Walden*.

http://librivox.org/walden-by-henry-david-thoreau/

Music

Listen to music from the 1956 movie score by Victor Young. This site has a music player with lyrical versions by singers such as Bing Crosby and Frank Sinatra:

http://jv.gilead.org.il/around.html

Jules Verne is mentioned in the lyrics of this song, "Globe Trotting Nelly Bly."

http://www.traditionalmusic.co.uk/old-time-music/003930.HTM

Video

Here is a brief video of Walden Pond with narration in Thoreau's own words.

http://excellence-in-literature.com/excellence-in-lit/lit-and-comp/e2-resources/walden-pond-video

Visual Arts

Here are sites with good photos of Walden Pond:

http://thoreau.eserver.org/pondpics.html

http://waldenproject.com/index.html

http://www.concord.org/~kathy/Walden/WaldenPond.html

Thoreau taught himself how to survey land, and created the first accurate survey of Walden Pond.

http://thoreau.eserver.org/survey.html

Music

Early American and British folk music were part of Thoreau's experience. You will find music for some typical songs at:

http://www.americanrevolution.org/songs.html

Listen to a variety of folk tunes at the site listed below. [Note: This site has background folk music that will start playing immediately—there is a pause button near the top of the page if this disturbs you.]

http://www.contemplator.com/folk.html

Places to Go

Concord, Massachusetts has been at the center of many historic events. The owners of Concord's Hawthorne Inn offer a sample itinerary highlighting area attractions you may wish to visit in this fascinating place rich in history, literature, and art.

http://www.concordmass.com/local-activities.php

Concord's Chamber of Commerce offers an extensive list of interesting places to visit and information about them. Hold your mouse over the "Visitor Info" link near the top of the page to see other links for more ways to explore the area.

http://concordchamberofcommerce.org/visitor-information/
concord-ma-visitor-information/

The Walden Woods Project "preserves the land, literature and legacy of the quintessential American author, philosopher, and naturalist, Henry David Thoreau, to foster an ethic of environmental stewardship and social responsibility." Their website contains a wealth of interesting information on Walden Woods, Thoreau, and the legacy of *Walden*. Read this brief article about Walden Woods, the setting of *Walden*.

http://www.walden.org/Explore/A_Sacred_Forest

This interactive map allows you to explore Walden Woods:

http://www.walden.org/Explore/Walden_Woods_Ecosystem

Assignment Schedule

Week 1

Read and explore context materials, and begin reading focus text. Follow the model in the Formats and Models chapter to write an Author Profile. Be sure to refer to your writer's handbook if you have questions about grammar, structure, or style.

Week 2

Complete one of the following assignments.

1- Imagine that you are one of the people living near Walden Pond. Write a letter to a friend describing Thoreau's project and including your own point of view about the idea. Be sure to include details about Thoreau's cabin, his meals, and most importantly, his ideas. Make it 200 words or more, and be sure to use vivid words and write in a conversational tone.

2- Write a Historical Period/Event Approach Paper following the format in the Formats and Models chapter, on American Romanticism in literature, art, and music. In addition to the context links I have provided you may use other resources such as your encyclopedia, the library, and quality Internet resources to complete this assignment.

Week 3

Begin drafting a 500-word paper on one of the topics below. I recommend that you follow the writing process outlined in the "How to Write an Essay" chapter, consulting the models in the Formats and Models chapter and your writer's handbook as needed.

1- Model: Literary Analysis Essay and MLA Format Model

Prompt: "The mass of men lead lives of quiet desperation." What evidence does Thoreau offer for this statement, and what are his solutions? If you like, you may also consider whether his ideas are really the solution to "lives of quiet desperation." Be sure to use quotations from the focus text to support your thesis.

2- Model: Literary Analysis Essay and MLA Format Model

Prompt: Write an essay comparing and contrasting how the philosophies of American Romanticism and American Transcendentalism are reflected in Thoreau's

Excellence in Literature: Reading and Writing through the Classics

work, and how ideas from each influenced his experiment at Walden Pond. Be sure to use quotations from the focus text to support your thesis.

For additional help, use your writer's handbook or refer to the "How to Write a Compare/Contrast Essay " article at the first URL below, and see a model at the second URL:

http://excellence-in-literature.com/resources-for-teaching/
how-to-write-a-compare-contrast-essay

http://excellence-in-literature.com/resources-for-teaching/
sample-compare-contrast-essay

Consider using a graphic organizer such as the Venn diagram to help organize your thoughts before you write the essay. Your writer's handbook may have instructions and models of many types of graphic organizers, or you may view some at my Pinterest board.

http://www.pinterest.com/janicecampbell/graphic-organizers/

Turn in the draft at the end of the week, so your writing mentor can evaluate it using the Content standards (Ideas/Concepts and Organization) on the rubric.

Week 4

Use the feedback on the rubric, along with the writing mentor's comments to revise your paper. Before turning in the final draft, be sure you have addressed any issues marked on the evaluation rubric, and verify that the thesis is clear and your essay is well-organized. Use your writer's handbook to check grammar or punctuation so that your essay will be free from mechanical errors. Turn in the essay at the end of the week so that the writing mentor can use the evaluation rubric in the "How to Evaluate" chapter to check your work.

Module 2.3

The Count of Monte Cristo by Alexandre Dumas (1802–1870)

> *. . . Never forget that until the day when God shall deign to*
> *reveal the future to man, all human wisdom is summed up in*
> *these two words,—"Wait and hope."*

—Alexandre Dumas

Focus Text

The Count of Monte Cristo by Alexandre Dumas

Honors Text

The Man in the Iron Mask or *The Three Musketeers* by Alexandre Dumas

Literary Period

Romantic

Module Focus

The Count of Monte Cristo is an early example of historical fiction. As you read, observe how Dumas skillfully blends historical fact with the fictional lives of his character to paint a realistic picture of life in nineteenth-century France.

Introduction

In this fast-moving adventure, young Edmond Dantès is unjustly imprisoned. He escapes, dramatically changed, after fourteen years and assumes the identity of the

Count of Monte Cristo in order to seek vengeance on four men who were responsible for his imprisonment. As he meets his goals, however, he finds that his revenge results in unintended consequences that affect people he never intended to harm.

Something to think about . . .

When Edmond Dantès escapes from prison, he is bent on revenge against the four men who wronged him. Because he believes that human justice would not be adequate punishment for them, he sees himself as a dispenser of divine justice. What are the unintended consequences of his revenge, and how does he feel when the revenge has been completed?

Be sure to notice . . .

The Count of Monte Cristo first appeared as a serial story, published in a popular French magazine. As you read through the book, notice how Dumas paces his story so that each scene ends with something unresolved, making it hard to put down the story. Can you imagine how hard it must have been to wait for a new installment of the story to find out what happened?

Context Resources

The Author's Life

Dumas was a prolific French writer who led an adventurous life. You may read a short biography of Alexandre Dumas in an encyclopedia or from your library.

This brief, interesting biography is followed by a list of further reading on the author's life, as well as a long (partial!) list of Dumas' works:

http://www.kirjasto.sci.fi/adumas1.htm

Dumas' racial heritage still stirs feelings in modern-day France: his grandmother was a black slave, and biographers differ as to how much his mixed race affected his life and career. This biography provides more detail about Dumas' mixed-race heritage:

http://www.intermix.org.uk/icons/icons_07_dumas.asp

If you like Dumas' work, you may want to read *The Fourth Musketeer: The Life of Alexandre Dumas* by J. Lucas-Dubreton, a full-length biography from 1928, available online.

http://www.cadytech.com/dumas/related/fourth_musketeer.php

You will find a great deal of useful information at the website of the Dumas Society. This English-language home page directs you to the many pages on the site that have been translated into English; some links you may see are available only in French.

http://www.dumaspere.com/pages/english/sommaire.html

Poetry

Victor Hugo is one of the best-known French Romantics, and is a contemporary of Alexandre Dumas. His poem, "Boaz Asleep," is a Romantic-style re-telling of the story of Boaz and Ruth.

http://excellence-in-literature.com/lit-and-comp/e2-resources/boaz-asleep-by-victor-hugo (English translation plus original French text)

Audio

If you wish to listen to the story, I recommend finding a professionally-produced version so that pronunciation of the French names and terms will be correct. Look at your local library or search for the book at:

www.audible.com

There is a free amateur version available online, but if you choose to listen to it, be aware that pronunciations may not be accurate.

http://librivox.org/the-count-of-monte-cristo-by-alexandre-dumas

Music

Scroll to the bottom of this page to listen to several well-done clips of military music from the age of Napoleon. Each is illustrated with a related work of art.

http://www.militaryheritage.com/sound.htm

Video

There is a 2002 movie version of the story with Richard Harris as Abbé Faria. I have not seen this but here is a link to a very positive review about it, and a link to more details about the movie. If you are able to rent it or find it at your local library, I recommend watching it after reading the focus text.

http://decentfilms.com/reviews/countofmontecristo2002.html

http://www.imdb.com/title/tt0245844/

You may watch a trailer here:

http://excellence-in-literature.com/lit-and-comp/e2-resources/
count-of-monte-cristo-trailer

You'll also find the 2002 film of *The Count of Monte Cristo* in several numbered
segments on YouTube. Here's the link to part one:

http://tinyurl.com/monte-cristo-1

Visual Arts

Eugène Delacroix (1798-1863) is one of the greatest artists of the French Romantic
movement, and just as Dumas inspired many writers after him, Delacroix
inspired painters in the Impressionist movement. Read about Delacroix and
view some of his work in an art history encyclopedia or at the Getty Museum
site below.

http://www.getty.edu/art/gettyguide/artMakerDetails?maker=408#top

Historic Context

The Count of Monte Cristo is set during the Napoleonic era, so it is important that
you have an idea of what the Napoleonic Wars were about, where they were
fought, and who was involved. There was more to that era than just the Battle of
Waterloo! You may consult your encyclopedia or library or visit the link below:

http://www.britannica.com/EBchecked/topic/219456/
French-revolutionary-and-Napoleonic-wars?anchor=ref171789

Places to Go

If you are fortunate enough to visit Port Marly in France, the Château de Monte
Cristo is the home Alexandre Dumas designed and had built for his family. You
can read about it at the first link below, and view a selection of photographs at
the second link:

http://www.dumaspere.com/pages/english/societe/chateau.html

http://www.dumaspere.com/pages/phototheque/montecristo.html

Photo captions are in French; to see each photo larger, click on the thumbnail, then
click on the image to close it.

You may view a virtual tour of the château here—this takes a little while to load, so be patient.

http://www.montecristo.specific-systems.net/

Practical information for planning a visit can be found at the official website for the Château de Monte Cristo:

http://www.chateau-monte-cristo.com/en/index.html

Assignment Schedule

Week 1

Read and explore context materials, and begin reading focus text. Follow the model in the Formats and Models chapter to write an Author Profile. Be sure to refer to your writer's handbook if you have questions about grammar, structure, or style.

Week 2

Write an approach paper, using the instructions and samples in the Formats and Models chapter. In addition to the context links I have provided, you may use other resources such as your encyclopedia, the library, and quality Internet resources to help you complete this assignment.

Week 3

Begin drafting a 500-word paper on one of the topics below. I recommend that you follow the writing process outlined in the "How to Write an Essay" chapter, consulting the models in the Formats and Models chapter and your writer's handbook as needed.

1- Model: Literary Analysis Essay and MLA Format Model

Prompt: After his imprisonment, Edmond Dantès centered his life around the pursuit of vengeance. Discuss how his ideas of justice and vengeance were shaped by his imprisonment, and how those ideas changed as he observed his own limitations and the unintended consequences of his revenge. If you like, you may also evaluate ways in which his ideas conform to Biblical principles of justice. Be sure to use brief quotations from the focus text and/or context works to support your thesis.

2- Model: Literary Analysis Essay and MLA Format Model

Prompt: Edmond Dantès' revenge on each man relates to that man's strongest motivating desire. For example, the greedy Danglars is ruined financially. Consider the revenge exacted on each man, and discuss ways in which their punishment fit the motivation for their crime against Dantès. Evaluate whether justice was served in each case, and support your position with appropriate quotes from the text.

Turn in the draft at the end of the week, so your writing mentor can evaluate it using the Content standards (Ideas/Concepts and Organization) on the rubric.

Week 4

Use the feedback on the rubric, along with the writing mentor's comments to revise your paper. Before turning in the final draft, be sure you have addressed any issues marked on the evaluation rubric, and verify that the thesis is clear and your essay is well-organized. Use your writer's handbook to check grammar or punctuation so that your essay will be free from mechanical errors. Turn in the essay at the end of the week so that the writing mentor can use the evaluation rubric in the "How to Evaluate" chapter to check your work.

Module 2.4

The Heart of Darkness by Joseph Conrad (1857–1924)

The belief in a supernatural source of evil is not necessary;
men alone are quite capable of every wickedness..

—Joseph Conrad

Focus Text

Heart of Darkness by Joseph Conrad

Honors Text

Manalive by G. K. Chesterton (1874-1936)

Literary Period

Modernist

Module Focus

Heart of Darkness is presented as a framed narrative—that is, a story told within a story. As you read, think about this technique, consider why Conrad may have used it and what it accomplishes. Would the book have been as effective if told in a different way, or from another point of view?

Introduction

In this module, you will read *Heart of Darkness* by Joseph Conrad, a powerful novella in which the narrator, Marlow, tells a story of his journey up the Congo River into the heart of Africa. The story addresses the issue of European colonialism, and is based on a life-changing trip that Conrad took in 1890.

Something to think about . . .

Joseph Conrad is an extraordinarily gifted writer, and despite his atheistic worldview, he was able to convey truth in his work. In *Heart of Darkness* he explores the idea that the evil that should be most feared is not evil from without, but from within. Although Conrad's view of man seems unalterably bleak, the protagonist Marlow's final act in the story (choosing to conceal Kurtz's last words from his fiancée) might be considered an act of mercy. What do you think? What do you think Conrad means by the heart of darkness?

Be sure to notice . . .

Conrad has been called a "prose poet" because of the evocative beauty of his writing. Fellow author T. E. Lawrence wrote that "He's absolutely the most haunting thing in prose that ever was: I wish I knew how every paragraph he writes (. . . they are all paragraphs: he seldom writes a single sentence . . .) goes on sounding in waves, like the note of a tenor bell, after it stops. It's not built in the rhythm of ordinary prose, but on something existing only in his head, and as he can never say what it is he wants to say, all his things end in a kind of hunger, a suggestion of something he cannot say or do or think. So his books always look bigger than they are." Be sure to notice how Conrad uses literary devices such as parallelism and metaphor to create the mood for each scene.

Context Resources

The Author's Life

Readings

The London Telegraph published an excellent article on the power and influence of *Heart of Darkness.*

http://www.telegraph.co.uk/culture/books/5708673/Joseph-Conrads-Heart-of- Darkness.html

If you have a *Norton Anthology of English Literature* that contains *Heart of Darkness,* read the brief biography of Joseph Conrad and the excellent introduction to *Heart of Darkness.*

The Author's Life

Look for Chris Fletcher's *Joseph Conrad*, part of the outstanding British *Writer's Lives* series. If you cannot find, it, another short biography will do. Conrad is such an outstanding writer, it is amazing to note that he did not learn English until he was an adult.

The Joseph Conrad Centre in Poland hosts an excellent online biography and time-line, with a number of good photographs.

http://conrad-centre.w.interia.pl/pages/conrad_life_en.htm

This brief vignette describes what inspired Conrad to write *Heart of Darkness*.

http://www.todayinliterature.com/stories.asp?Event_Date=9/6/1890

Read this overview of the tragic history of King Leopold and his exploitation of the Belgian Congo at the Constitutional Rights Foundation.

http://www.crf-usa.org/bill-of-rights-in-action/
bria-16-2-a-king-leopold-s-heart-of-darkness

Mark Twain was deeply opposed to colonialism and lent his support to the Congo Reform Association by writing a satirical pamphlet called "King Leopold's Soliloquy," in which King Leopold tries to defend his activities in the Congo.

http://diglib1.amnh.org/articles/kls/index.html

Sir Arthur Conan Doyle, author of the Sherlock Holmes mysteries, also supported the Congo Reform Association and wrote a concise but vivid overview of the situation, complete with eyewitness accounts of atrocities. Read at least the introduction and first four chapters; the remainder is optional, though it would be very helpful in understanding *Heart of Darkness*.

http://www.kongo-kinshasa.de/dokumente/lekture/crime_of_congo.pdf

Yale University's Genocide Study Project has posted a scholarly overview of what happened in the Belgian Congo. Because this may be disturbing, it is optional reading.

http://www.yale.edu/gsp/colonial/belgian_congo/

If this historic period interests you, your local library should have more resources on the Belgian Congo, King Leopold, and colonialism.

Poetry

Thomas Stearns Eliot (1888-1965) was a contemporary of Joseph Conrad, and is known to have read Conrad's work. A great Modernist poet, he converted to Christianity mid-way through his career. At The Poetry Archive, you may read this brief biography of T. S. Eliot, and if you like, listen to one or more audio recordings of his work.

http://www.poetryarchive.org/poetryarchive/singlePoet.do?poetId=7069

"The Hollow Men" by T. S. Eliot alludes to *Heart of Darkness* and evokes a similar mood. Read the Introduction and essay on "Allusions" at the first link; then read the annotated poem at the second link. The poem is on the left side of the page and the annotations, which will help you understand the poem, are on the right. Click on an underlined word in the poem on the left to bring the corresponding annotation to the top of the right-hand column.

http://www.aduni.org/~heather/occs/honors/Default.htm

http://www.aduni.org/~heather/occs/honors/Poem.htm

Listen to T. S. Eliot reading his own poem, "The Hollow Men." His poignant, dramatic recitation will help you grasp the poem in a way that is not possible through simply reading it. Poetry is meant to be heard!

http://excellence-in-literature.com/lit-and-comp/e2-resources/
the-hollow-men-read-aloud-by-t-s-eliot

Audio

You can find *Heart of Darkness* on CD or MP3 from your library or www.Audible.com, or get the free audio download from Librivox.

http://librivox.org/heart-of-darkness-by-joseph-conrad/

At the Mercury Theatre website, you can listen to a short dramatized version of *Heart of Darkness* produced by Orson Welles and John Houseman. Scroll down to the November 6, 1938 show to find it. (This is not a substitute for reading the whole book.)

http://www.mercurytheatre.info/

Music

Heart of Darkness is a well-reviewed chamber opera in one act by Tarik O'Regan, with an English-language libretto by artist Tom Phillips. Visit the link below to watch an interview with the composer and see a student-produced musical on the same topic.

http://excellence-in-literature.com/lit-and-comp/e2-resources/heart-of-darkness-opera

This recording of Vincent Persichetti "The Hollow Men," for trumpet & string orchestra, Op. 25" evokes the dark mood of both *Heart of Darkness* and "The Hollow Men." You may enjoy listening to this as you read.

http://excellence-in-literature.com/excellence-in-lit/lit-and-comp/e2-resources/hollow-men-music

Video

I have no recommended movie version of this story. "Apocalypse Now" is a movie version of *Heart of Darkness*, and because of its box office success, you will often find it recommended in connection with the study of the book. It is R-rated, and I do not recommend it.

Visual Arts

This excellent site offers photos, artwork, videos, and maps of many places and things in *Heart of Darkness*. These are organized to move chronologically through the book, so you can supplement your reading with illustrations and annotations.

http://www.bookdrum.com/books/heart-of-darkness/9780140186529/book-marks-1-25.html?bookId=284

Here is a modern art installation inspired by *Heart of Darkness*. Do you think the mood of this piece captures the mood of the story?

http://www.artnet.com/artwork/424743693/1029/cornelia-parker-heart-of-darkness.html

Look at this zoomable map of the Belgian Congo at the World Digital Library.

http://www.wdl.org/en/item/59/

The *CIA World Factbook* has a current map and good background information on the current Democratic Republic of the Congo.

https://www.cia.gov/library/publications/the-world-factbook/geos/cg.html

Places to Go

Joseph Conrad was born in the town of Berdychiv in Poland, and there are several sites there that honor his life and work. Other memorials may be found in Australia, San Francisco, Singapore, and Vologda, Russia.

Assignment Schedule

Week 1

Read and explore context materials, and begin reading focus text. Follow the model in the Formats and Models chapter to write an Author Profile. Be sure to refer to your writer's handbook if you have questions about grammar, structure, or style.

Week 2

Write a Historical Period/Event Approach Paper on King Leopold's reign over the Belgian Congo. You will find the format and a sample paper in the "Formats and Models" chapter. In addition to the context links I have provided, you may use other resources such as your encyclopedia, the library, and quality Internet resources to complete this assignment.

Week 3

Begin drafting a 550-word paper on one of the topics below. I recommend that you follow the writing process outlined in the "How to Write an Essay" chapter, consulting the models in the Formats and Models chapter and your writer's handbook as needed.

1- Model: Literary Analysis Essay and MLA Format Model

Prompt: Darkness and light are powerful symbols throughout the story. Consider how they are used, and discuss their meanings and how or whether that meaning changes in various contexts. Provide specific examples to support your thesis.

2- Model: Literary Analysis Essay and MLA Format Model

- Psalm 139
God is light

Prompt: Consider another example of colonialism—the settlement of the Americas by European powers. Think about an event such as the settlement of the English in Virginia or the Westward Movement and compare the events of this colonization with the colonization of the Belgian Congo as depicted by Conrad. What were the colonizers actions toward the natives, and how did the attitude and actions of the natives toward the colonizers change over time?

Turn in the draft at the end of the week, so your writing mentor can evaluate it using the Content standards (Ideas/Concepts and Organization) on the rubric.

Week 4

Use the feedback on the rubric along with the writing mentor's comments to revise your paper. Before turning in the final draft, be sure you have addressed any issues marked on the evaluation rubric and verify that the thesis is clear and your essay is well-organized. Use your writer's handbook to check grammar or punctuation so that your essay will be free from mechanical errors. Turn in the essay at the end of the week so that the writing mentor can use the evaluation rubric in the "How to Evaluate" chapter to check your work.

Module 2.5

Till We Have Faces by C. S. Lewis (1898-1965)

A man can no more diminish God's glory by refusing to worship Him than a lunatic can put out the sun by scribbling the word, "darkness" on the walls of his cell.

—C. S. Lewis

Focus Text

Till We Have Faces by C. S. Lewis

Honors Text

The Screwtape Letters by C. S. Lewis

Optional Reading for Parents

The Four Loves by C. S. Lewis: This is an advanced study of the nature of love, and is very helpful in understanding the four basic types of love: affection, friendship, eros, charity. Parents may want to read this so they can help their students better understand the types of love seen in *Till We Have Faces*.

Literary Period

Modern Myth

Module Focus

The story is narrated by Orual, an unreliable narrator (see Glossary) with an agenda. As you read Part I, watch for clues that things are not exactly as she portrays them.

Introduction

In *Till We Have Faces*, C. S. Lewis retells the myth of Cupid and Psyche from the perspective of Orual, one of Psyche's sisters. She narrates the story in an effort to justify her actions toward her sister, and to show how unfairly the gods have treated her. Her writing, and the reading aloud of her words, ultimately helps Orual to see herself as she really is and to see what she has done to others. When, through a series of visions, she faces and accepts the truth she has tried to escape, she is redeemed.

Something to think about . . .

Lewis believed that one of the best ways to share truth was by placing it in an unexpected setting. In this way, the essential truth of the story would reach the listener's heart, as it did in Scripture when the prophet Nathan told King David the story of the rich man who sacrificed the poor man's lamb (II Samuel 12). Placing the story in another context removed all David's rationale for his sin and revealed the true picture of what he had done. In *Till We Have Faces*, Lewis tells the story of Orual to illustrate the nature of true agape love.

Another thing to think about: Anytime you have a conflicted or confusing situation or emotion, try writing down everything you are thinking (use a private journal so that you can be absolutely truthful). Read aloud to yourself what you have written, and it will help you see where your thoughts are not true or accurate.

Be sure to notice . . .

Orual's veil seems to symbolize her self-deception and lack of true personal identity. Until she removes it and has a visible face, she is separated not only from other people, but also from a relationship with God.

Context Resources

Readings

Thomas Bulfinch's retelling of the original Cupid and Psyche myth, from his book *The Age of Fable; or, Stories of Gods and Heroes* (1855), will help you to understand Lewis's version. You may find this resource at either of the links below.

With notes on the story's origin by Dr. Ashliman (University of Pittsburgh):

http://www.pitt.edu/~dash/cupid.html

In a more simple format:

http://excellence-in-literature.com/lit-and-comp/e2-resources/cupid-and-psyche-myth-told-by-bulfinch-in-age-of-fable

Dr. Bruce L. Edwards, a C. S. Lewis scholar and minister, maintains the CS Lewis Review, with articles, resources, and links related to C. S. Lewis and the Inklings. Browse through and read anything you like, but do not miss "A Way into *Till We Have Faces.*"

http://www.cslewisreview.org/2010/01/a-way-into-till-we-have-faces/

"Reason and Imagination in C. S. Lewis: A Study of *Till We Have Faces*" by Peter J. Schakel, a professor at Hope College, is available online if you need extra help understanding the story.

http://www.hope.edu/academic/english/about/facultyprofiles/schakel/tillwehavefaces/reason.htm

Professor Henry Karlson has written a helpful overview of *Till We Have Faces.*

http://houseoftheinklings.blogspot.com/2006/12/till-we-have-faces.html

If you enjoy Lewis's works, you will find that the *C. S. Lewis Reader's Encyclopedia* (Ed. by Jeffrey D. Schultz and John G. West Jr.) is a superb resource for understanding his life and works.

The Mythopoeic Society provides good overview of the Inklings and their work.

http://www.mythsoc.org/inklings

Minister and scholar Richard James shares three presentations on C. S. Lewis and his works, given in honor of the 100th anniversary of Lewis's birth.

http://www.crlamppost.org/centpresent.htm

Invitation to the Classics offers a brief overview of Lewis's life and the themes and background of his popular epistolary novel, *The Screwtape Letters.*

The Author's Life

You may read any good, brief biography of C. S. Lewis and/or his autobiography, *Surprised by Joy* (one of my favorite autobiographies). Many good full-length biographies are also available, and are generally suitable for all ages.

This brief biography will give you a quick overview of C. S. Lewis's life and works:

http://www.cslewiscollege.org/c-s-lewis/

Do not miss this fascinating interview with Douglas Gresham, one of Lewis's step-sons, in which he provides a wonderful account of Lewis's life and personality:

http://www.duncanentertainment.com/gresham.php

The C. S. Lewis Institute offers a variety of excellent articles on Lewis's life and works.

http://www.cslewisinstitute.org/Articles_About_CS_Lewis

This BBC website offers an extensive biography of C. S. Lewis, along with information on many of his books:

http://www.bbc.co.uk/religion/religions/christianity/people/cslewis_1.shtml

Here is a chronological outline of Lewis's life.

http://www.cslewis.org/resources/chronocsl.html

Poetry

C. S. Lewis loved poetry, and these are some of the poets and poems that influenced his life and works.

"The Prelude" is William Wordsworth's poetic autobiography, considered his greatest poetic work. At the first link, thirteen members of the Faculty of English at the University of Cambridge stage a live, online reading marathon of all thirteen books. I suggest listening to Book Eighth - *Retrospect: Love of Nature Leading to Love of Mankind* or another book of your choice. At the second link is the full text of the poem.

http://www.english.cam.ac.uk/multimedia/wordsworth/

http://www.bartleby.com/145/ww287.html

Read at least five poems from *The Temple* by George Herbert. Be sure to include "Evensong" and "Love I, II, and III."

http://www.luminarium.org/sevenlit/herbert/herbbib.htm

If you enjoy George Herbert's devotional poetry, you will want to read *Working it Out: Growing Spiritually with the Poetry of George Herbert* by Joseph L. Womack. This delightful volume offers a minister's explication of selected Herbert poems. For each poem he covers The Big Picture, The Parts of the Picture, The Parts of the Picture Come Together, Reflections, and Scriptures for Further Reflection. It is not just a devotional guide; it is also a very helpful example of how to get the most from reading poetry. Highly recommended. NOTE: It has gone out of print, but we have received permission to republish it, and hope to have it available by the end of 2014.

Audio

The audio version of *Till We Have Faces* is available on CD or MP3 through Amazon.com or Audible.com. This will be very helpful for auditory learners.

Dr. Peter Kreeft offers an insightful 74-minute lecture on *Till We Have Faces*. I highly recommend this. The recording starts a little abruptly—keep listening!

http://www.peterkreeft.com/audio/16_cslewis-till-we-have-faces.htm

Into the Wardrobe, a C. S. Lewis web site, offers a number of fascinating audio clips. You can hear Lewis himself, as well as readings (by others) from the Narnia series.

http://cslewis.drzeus.net/multimedia/audio.html

Richard James, a minister and scholar, offers several interesting audio presentations on C.S. Lewis at his website.

http://www.crlamppost.org/audio.htm

Music

You may want to listen to the *Cupid and Psyche Suite* by Lord Berners (Gerald Hugh Tyrwhitt-Wilson 1883–1950) as you read. You may sample or purchase the music on the Classics Online site.

http://www.classicsonline.com/catalogue/product.aspx?pid=1397

Video

The story of C. S. Lewis and Joy Davidman Gresham is told in *Shadowlands*, a 1993 movie with Anthony Hopkins as Lewis. You may read a brief review on the Decent Films Guide website.

http://decentfilms.com/reviews/shadowlands.html

You may watch the trailer here:

http://excellence-in-literature.com/lit-and-comp/e2-resources/shadowlands-trailer

Decent Films Guide also offers a selection of good articles on the *Chronicles of Narnia* movies. If you have not seen these, you may enjoy them.

http://decentfilms.com/search?title=narnia&search=Quick+Search

Till We Have Faces has been adapted into a well-reviewed play, and would be worth seeing if it comes to a theatre near you.

Visual Arts

Photos of The Kilns, C. S. Lewis's home and garden, plus links to photos of other important places in Lewis's life:

http://www.headington.org.uk/history/buildings/kilns.htm

Interesting Facts

Lewis and fellow author Aldous Huxley died on the same day that John F. Kennedy was assassinated. With this interesting fact in mind, Dr. Peter Kreeft has written *Between Heaven and Hell: A Dialog Somewhere Beyond Death with John F. Kennedy, C. S. Lewis & Aldous Huxley*. It is well worth reading.

After the death of his wife, Joy, Lewis wrote *A Grief Observed*. It was such a personal book that he used a pseudonym, but after friends kept recommending that he read it, he allowed it to be republished under his own name.

Places to Visit

The C. S. Lewis Foundation offers a walking tour to many significant C. S. Lewis sites in Oxford, England. This tour includes the Eagle and Child Pub, where the Inklings met; and Magdalen College, where he taught.

http://www.cslewis.org/resource/walkguide/

Should you be planning a visit to Oxford, The Kilns offers tours upon request:

http://www.cslewis.org/programs/kilns/kilnstour.htm

Assignment Schedule

Week 1

Begin reading the context resources and the novel, and follow the model in the Formats and Models chapter to write an Author Profile. Be sure to refer to your writer's handbook if you have questions about grammar, structure, or style.

Week 2

Choose one of the following short assignments:

1- Retell the Cupid and Psyche myth as a story that takes place in a modern setting.

2- Write a brief summary of the original Cupid and Psyche myth, and briefly compare the original myth with Lewis's retelling. This should be no more than one page long.

Week 3

Complete context resources, and begin drafting a 500-word essay on the topic below. I recommend that you follow the writing process outlined in the "How to Write an Essay" chapter, consulting the models in the Formats and Models chapter and your writer's handbook as needed.

Model: Literary Analysis Essay and MLA Format Model

Prompt: Orual begins her book to tell her side of the story in order to justify herself. Consider what happens when she finally has the opportunity to present her case to the gods. Discuss the significance in the change she perceived in her book, the numerous repetitions of the story, and the silence that followed. What does the statement, "The complaint was the answer," mean? What does Orual learn about herself and about love, and what was the final answer she finally found? Be sure to support your thesis with appropriate quotes from the text.

Turn in the draft at the end of the week, so your writing mentor can evaluate it using the Content standards (Ideas/Concepts and Organization) on the rubric.

Week 4

Use the feedback on the rubric along with the writing mentor's comments to revise your paper. Before turning in the final draft, be sure you have addressed any issues marked on the evaluation rubric, and verify that the thesis is clear and your essay is well-organized. Use your writer's handbook to check grammar or punctuation so that your essay will be free from mechanical errors. Turn in the essay at the end of the week so that the writing mentor can use the evaluation rubric in the "How to Evaluate" chapter to check your work.

Module 2.6

Death Comes for the Archbishop by Willa Cather (1873-1947)

We come and go, but the land is always here.
And the people who love it and understand it are the people who own it for a little while.

—Willa Cather

Focus Text

Death Comes for the Archbishop by Willa Cather

Honors Texts

Country of the Pointed Firs by Sarah Orne Jewett

Literary Period

Modernist/Regional

Module Focus

In *Death Comes for the Archbishop,* you will observe how Cather paints the books's setting and characters using vivid, specific language. You will also observe some of the conventions of regional and of episodic fiction.

Introduction

Death Comes for the Archbishop is a episodic narrative based upon the life and experiences of Catholic Archbishop Jean Baptiste Lamy in the territory of New Mexico during the last part of the 19th century. Cather's character, Jean Latour, along with fellow priest Joseph Vaillant, revitalizes the Catholic Church in the Southwest after nearly three centuries of neglect. Cather tells the story in distinct scenes, rather than as a chronological narrative, and each carefully chosen episode builds the reader's picture of the silent land and the priests, Indians, and others who move over the landscape.

Something to think about . . .

Although Cather was not a Roman Catholic, she chose to tell her story of the American Southwest through the character of a priest. This is logical, because a priest's life would touch the lives of a wide variety of people, providing the broadest possible picture of the Southwest at that point in history. What would the story have been like if told through the eyes of Jacinto or Dona Isabella?

Be sure to notice . . .

Willa Cather is best known for writing novels in which the setting is part of the story. Reading one of her novels is almost like taking a journey, because her word pictures are so vivid that the reader is able to see what her characters see. Notice how the setting of each scene contributes to the mood of the story and affects the actions of each character.

Context Resources

Readings

This interesting article by author Kathleen Norris is a good introduction to Willa Cather and her work, and will help you understand what makes her work significant. It is included in the PBS "American Masters" series.

http://www.pbs.org/wnet/americanmasters/episodes/willa-cather/about-willa-cather/549/

The Spanish Bishop in the opening scene mentions that his knowledge of America was chiefly drawn from the writings of James Fenimore Cooper. To become familiar with Cooper's writing, you may read "The Lake Gun," a short story:

http://excellence-in-literature.com/excellence-in-lit/lit-and-comp/e2-resources/the-lake-gun-by-james-fenimore-cooper

Other authors mentioned in the story are Blaise Pascal, Saint Augustine, and Mme. de Sévigné. Look them up in your encyclopedia or online, and think about why these particular writers may have been meaningful to the author or the story.

The Author's Life

Look for *Writer of the Plains: A Story About Willa Cather* by Thomas Streissguth, a Creative Minds Biography for middle-grade readers, at your library.

The Willa Cather Foundation website contains a brief biography, photos, quotes and other information about and by the author.

http://www.willacather.org

The *Outline of American Literature* offers an overview of literary movements. It is interesting and useful, and you will find Willa Cather's work discussed under the heading "Two Women Regional Novelists."

http://excellence-in-literature.com/excellence-in-lit/american-lit/e3-resources/
ch-5-outline-of-american-literature-by-kathryn-vanspanckeren

Poetry

Amy Lowell is a poet who, like Cather, beautifully captures the mood of a specific time and place. Read the following selections from an anthology or at one of the links below.

- "A London Thoroughfare. 2 A.M."
- "Bath"
- "Midday and Afternoon"
- "The Garden by Moonlight"

http://excellence-in-literature.com/lit-and-comp/e2-resources/amy-lowell-poetry

Edward Arlington Robinson is another notable poet of the era. His poem, "Mr. Flood's Party," is particularly moving.

http://excellence-in-literature.com/lit-and-comp/e2-resources/
mr-floods-party-by-edwin-arlington-robinson

For a regional touch, read "Passing Through Albuquerque" by John Balaban.

http://www.poets.org/viewmedia.php/prmMID/16486

Audio

Death Comes for the Archbishop was recorded on audio-cassette many years ago, and may be available at your library. There is no other audio version currently available.

Music

Among the composers mentioned in *Death Comes for the Archbishop* are Giuseppe Verdi, Johann Sebastian Bach, and Stephen Foster. Your library may have works by these composers, or you can listen online:

http://excellence-in-literature.com/lit-and-comp/e2-resources/
composers-in-death-comes-for-the-archbishop

Visit the *On Classical* website to listen to or download albums of music by Verdi and Bach (click on the "Composers" link at top left, then find them in the alphabetical listing).

http://www.onclassical.com

You will find a large collection of Stephen Foster's music, as well as information about his life and works at this website below.

http://www.stephen-foster-songs.de

Video

Willa Cather: The Road Is All is a PBS documentary of Cather and her work from the American Masters Series. I have not watched it, but it is well-reviewed, so may be worth watching. You may be able to find the video at your local library, or you can order it from the PBS store or Amazon.com.

http://www.shopthirteen.org/product/show/29443

You may learn about Willa Cather's letters in this video from the University of Nebraska:

http://excellence-in-literature.com/lit-and-comp/e2-resources/willa-cather-letters

Visual Arts

Dr. Kathleen Nichols from the English Department at Pittsburgh State University has posted a page of art related to *Death Comes for the Archbishop*, annotated with quotes from Cather's work.

http://arcadiasystems.org/academia/cathart5.html

Artists mentioned *Death Comes for the Archbishop* include El Greco, Raphael, Titian, Jean-Georges Vibert, and Henri Fantin-Latour. If you own a copy of *The Annotated Mona Lisa* or other art history book, study the work of these artists. If not, read about each one in an encyclopedia and look at the paintings on the page below. Think about the work of each painter in the context of *Death Comes for the Archbishop*. Why do you think Cather might have chosen to mention these particular artists?

http://excellence-in-literature.com/lit-and-comp/e2-resources/
art-in-death-comes-for-the-archbishop

Historic and Geographic Context

Read about the history of New Mexico, paying particular attention to the 19th century, in your encyclopedia, a book from the library, or at the New Mexico Digital History project.

http://dev.newmexicohistory.org/home_html.php

In order to visualize the setting of *Death Comes for the Archbishop*, it is helpful to see New Mexico. The easiest way to do this is visit your library or bookstore and browse through a book about the state. If you can not do this, view Google image results for New Mexico scenery.

http://goo.gl/Y3G10

Using a map of the Americas, locate all the places the priests traveled, and consider their methods of travel (walking, horseback, boat, wagon train, etc).

Places to Go

You can tour Willa Cather's first (childhood) home in Red Bluff, Nebraska either in person or online at the Willa Cather foundation website, below. Click on each room to see photographs and learn more about them; Willa Cather's bedroom features wallpaper she purchased and hung when she was a teenager. Very interesting!

http://www.willacather.org/cather-tours/cather-home-tour

You can visit the stunningly beautiful Cathedral Basilica of Saint Francis of Assisi in Santa Fe, New Mexico. It was built around the old adobe church by Archbishop Jean Baptiste Lamy, the real person upon whom Cather based the character of Jean Latour. The first link provides a bit of history about the cathedral, and the second offers a virtual tour.

http://www.cbsfa.org/parish-life/about

http://www.cbsfa.org/89

Assignment Schedule

Week 1

Begin reading the context resources and the novel, and follow the model in the Formats and Models chapter to write an Author Profile. Be sure to refer to your writer's handbook if you have questions about grammar, structure, or style.

Week 2

Write a scene from the perspective of a stranger arriving at your home for the first time. Use Cather's writing style to describe your home and its surroundings in vivid, specific language. If you have difficulty getting started, type out a few descriptive passages from the book. This will help you understand Cather's rhythm and pacing, as well as her word choices. You can do this with any good author, and it will help you become a better writer.

Week 3

Begin drafting a 550-word paper on one of the topics below. I recommend that you follow the writing process outlined in the "How to Write an Essay" chapter, consulting the models in the Formats and Models chapter and your writer's handbook as needed.

1- Model: Literary Analysis Essay and MLA Format Model

Prompt: One of the major challenges facing Bishop Jean Marie Latour when he arrives in New Mexico is gaining the trust of the people he came to serve. What were the difficulties that made this so hard, and how was he able to overcome them? Support your thesis with appropriate examples from the text.

2- Model: Literary Analysis Essay and MLA Format Model

Prompt: What role does the landscape play in the story? In what ways can it be seen as a character? Be sure to use specific quotes and examples from the text to support your ideas.

Turn in the draft at the end of the week, so your writing mentor can evaluate it using the Content standards (Ideas/Concepts and Organization) on the rubric.

Week 4

Use the feedback on the rubric along with the writing mentor's comments to revise your paper. Before turning in the final draft, be sure you have addressed any issues marked on the evaluation rubric, and verify that the thesis is clear and your essay is well-organized. Use your writer's handbook to check grammar or punctuation so that your essay will be free from mechanical errors. Turn in the essay at the end of the week so that the writing mentor can use the evaluation rubric in the "How to Evaluate" chapter to check your work.

Module 2.7

Julius Caesar by William Shakespeare (1564–1616)

> When beggars die, there are no comets seen;
> The heavens themselves blaze forth the death of princes.
>
> —Act 2, Scene 2

Focus Text

Julius Caesar by William Shakespeare

You will need the text, as well as a video, of this play. You can find it in a Shakespeare anthology, as a stand-alone book, or in some editions of the *Norton Anthology of English Literature*. It is very helpful to use an annotated version such as the one published by Norton.

You may also download the text as a plain text file if you need multiple copies for a performance:

http://www.gutenberg.org/dirs/etext97/1ws2410.txt

Honors Texts

King John by William Shakespeare

Literary Period

Renaissance

Module Focus

The real Julius Caesar was considered to be one of Rome's best orators and writers (his war memoirs are still studied in Latin classes), and Shakespeare is considered one of the supreme English prose stylists, so it seems appropriate that in this unit we focus on the use of rhetoric and irony (see Glossary if you are not sure of the meaning of these words).

Introduction

This historical fiction drama is loosely based on the assassination of Julius Caesar of Rome. Marcus Brutus, Caesar's close friend, is persuaded by Cassius to join a conspiracy to assassinate Caesar because they believed he was becoming too powerful. Caesar's courage and confidence work against him, and he is murdered.

The conspirators briefly take charge, but at Caesar's funeral, his friend Mark Antony gives a speech that turns the tide of opinion against the conspirators, and they flee. Antony, along with Caesar's grandnephew and adopted son, Octavius, and Lepidus, a wealthy banker, form a group called the Second Triumvirate, and war ensues. As you read the play and the context readings, think about the differences between the real-life story and Shakespeare's drama. Why do you think he told the story as he did?

Something to think about . . .

This play contains many examples of persuasive rhetoric. Note particularly the speeches in which Cassius persuades Brutus to join the conspiracy against Caesar, Brutus speaks to persuade the people that the slaying of Caesar was for their own good, and Mark Antony speaks to turn the people against Brutus and Cassius. In the latter two speeches (Act 3, Scene 2), note the different techniques that each speaker used, and note how the crowd responds to each.

Be sure to notice . . .

In Mark Antony's speech, he used irony to achieve his goal. When he said "Brutus is an honourable man," he spoke the truth about Brutus's reputation. What else did he say that made these words seem to mean something different? How does Antony's speech differ in style from Brutus's, and what does this seem to indicate about the character of each man?

Context Resources

Readings

Here is a quick overview of the events in the play. Read this before you read or watch the play so that you will have a better understanding as you experience it.

http://absoluteshakespeare.com/guides/summaries/caesar/julius_caesar_summary. htm

The introduction to Julius Caesar in the *Norton Shakespeare* book (by Stephen Greenblatt, et al.) is another excellent resource. If you have access to this anthology, read this introduction before reading the play.

This delightful introduction to Shakespeare's grammar will help you understand his writings more easily.

http://www.bardweb.net/grammar/grammar.html

The *Eyewitness to History* site offers a look at the assassination of Caesar from the perspective of those who were alive at the time.

http://www.eyewitnesstohistory.com/caesar2.htm

Use this helpful online study guide to deepen your understanding of the plot, characters, and themes of *Julius Caesar.*

http://www.cummingsstudyguides.net/xJuliusCae.html

Here is a translated online version of *The Gallic Wars* by Julius Caesar. You do not have to read the whole thing, but at least read the first seven chapters. They're extremely short, but interesting, and will give you an idea of Caesar's storytelling style.

http://classics.mit.edu/Caesar/gallic.1.1.html

The Author's Life

Shakespeare by Peter Chrisp: This Eyewitness book from Dorling Kindersley publishers is a superb guide to Shakespeare and his plays. Like most Eyewitness books, it is lavishly illustrated, and both entertaining and informative.

The Shakespeare Resource Center provides a good introductory biography of Shakespeare, as well as many other useful resources.

http://www.bardweb.net/man.html

Timeline of important events in Shakespeare's life:

http://absoluteshakespeare.com/trivia/timeline/timeline.htm

The Seven Ages of Shakespeare's Life:

http://ise.uvic.ca/Library/SLT/life/lifesubj.html

Who wrote Shakespeare's works? Now that you have read about Shakespeare, you should know that there is an ongoing controversy about who actually wrote all his works. The Shakespeare Oxford site offers "A Beginner's Guide to the Shakespeare Authorship Problem." Do not miss this!

http://www.shakespeare-oxford.com/?p=35

Poetry

Shakespeare wrote many sonnets, including "Shall I Compare Thee to a Summer's Day?" Read and/or listen to it at the EIL website.

http://excellence-in-literature.com/poetry-2/
shall-i-compare-thee-to-a-summers-day-by-william-shakespeare

Visit this page to read poetry from Shakespeare's contemporaries, including Queen Elizabeth, Sir Philip Sydney, and Sir Walter Raleigh.

http://excellence-in-literature.com/excellence-in-lit/british-lit/e4-resources/
poetry-by-shakespeare-contemporaries

Audio

Your library may have this play on CD, but you can also download it free at Librivox (this is an amateur production, so check your library first).

http://librivox.org/julius-caesar-by-william-shakespeare/

Listen to this three-minute "CramCast" for some very helpful information about Shakespeare and the play.

http://media.wiley.com/assets/1536/60/cliffs_ep03.mp3

Music

Film Score Monthly offers a fascinating look at the ideas behind the composition of the musical score for the 1953 film version of *Julius Caesar*. Read this before you watch the film, as it will help you understand it better.

http://www.filmscoremonthly.com/cds/detail.cfm/cdID/299/

George Frideric Handel wrote the opera, *Julius Caesar in Egypt*. You can hear San Diego OperaTalk's Nick Reveles discuss the opera, Handel, baroque opera, and musical ornamentation in an interesting episode of San Diego OperaTalk. Nothing can compare to being at a live opera, but this is a decent introduction (listen to the other videos in this series if you enjoyed this). Listen to this first, then to the arias linked below.

http://excellence-in-literature.com/excellence-in-lit/lit-and-comp/e2-resources/operatalk-on-handels-julius-caesar-in-egypt

Aria *"L'angue offeso mai riposa"*:

http://excellence-in-literature.com/excellence-in-lit/lit-and-comp/e2-resources/julius-caesar-handel-opera-aria-langue-offeso-mai-riposa

Aria *"Se pieta di me non senti"*:

http://excellence-in-literature.com/excellence-in-lit/lit-and-comp/e2-resources/julius-caesar-handel-opera-aria-se-pieta-di-me-non-senti

Video

You may find the Oscar-winning 1953 black and white *Julius Caesar* at your library. It is helpful to have the written play with you as you are watching, as this will help you keep up with the fast-paced dialogue. You may want to watch it more than once, as Shakespearean English can be a bit hard to understand at first.

http://excellence-in-literature.com/lit-and-comp/e2-resources/julius-caesar-video

Watch the video of Mark Antony's speech at least twice. Observe how he uses irony to persuade his listeners, and carefully note the pacing and placement of each point. This is an example of rhetoric in action. If you are unable to watch this sin the 1953 film, you may watch another performance of the speech featured at the link below:

http://excellence-in-literature.com/excellence-in-lit/lit-and-comp/e2-resources/mark-antony-funeral-oration-shakespeare-julius-caesar.

Visual Arts

Photographs and artwork will help you visualize Shakespeare's life, as well as the setting and characters of Julius Caesar.

Shakespeare Birthplace Photographs

http://www.shakespeare.org.uk/visit-the-houses/shakespeares-birthplace.html

"The Death of Caesar" by Jean-Léon Gérôme, the "Assassination of Julius Caesar" by Vincenzo Camuccini, and others can be seen on the Julius Caesar page on the EIL website.

http://excellence-in-literature.com/lit-and-comp/e2-resources/caesar-artwork

"The Ides of March" by Edward John Poynter 1883

http://english.emory.edu/classes/Shakespeare_Illustrated/Poynter.Ides.html

Historic Context

Look at your local library for the Eyewitness book *Ancient Rome* by Simon James. This will give you a good overview of the things that Caesar might have encountered during his lifetime.

Use your encyclopedia to read about the Roman Empire, Julius Caesar, and the Ides of March, then read this vivid account of what really happened on the Ides of March in BC 44.

http://penelope.uchicago.edu/~grout/encyclopaedia_romana/calendar/ides.html

Virtual Globe Theatre

Clemson University offers a virtual tour of the Globe Theatre. This is very interesting, but it works best with a high-speed Internet connection. If you do not have high-speed at home, you can probably view this site on a computer at your local library.

http://virtual.clemson.edu/caah/shakespr/VRGLOBE/index.php

Assignment Schedule

Week 1

Begin reading the context resources and watch the Julius Caesar video (the drama comes alive when seen, as Shakespeare intended). Follow the model in the Formats and Models chapter to write an Author Profile. If you studied *Introduction to Literature* and have already done an author profile for Shakespeare, write a profile of Julius Caesar, using the same format as the Author Profile, but changing "Best Known Works" to "Most Significant Accomplishments." Be sure to refer to your writer's handbook if you have questions about grammar, structure, or style.

Week 2

Read *Julius Caesar*. As you read through the play, write a brief summary (1-3 sentences) of each scene. Number each summary with the scene number so that you can use it to find examples you wish to quote in your essay.

Copy the speeches of Brutus and Mark Antony in Act 3, Scene 2. Leave out all the interjected comments of the plebeians, and copy only the words of the two speeches. You may type or write these—do not copy and paste. The act of copying will help you understand and absorb the rhythm and structure of well-crafted rhetoric. It will also help you grasp the immensity of Shakespeare's gift. This is important, so do not skip it.

Week 3

Begin drafting a 600-word paper on one of the topics below. I recommend that you follow the writing process outlined in the "How to Write an Essay" chapter, consulting the models in the Formats and Models chapter and your writer's handbook as needed.

1- Model: Literary Analysis Essay and MLA Format Model

Prompt: Is Caesar or Brutus the hero in this play? Caesar dies, but his power and name continues, while Brutus is a noble man whose tragic flaw leads to his downfall. Decide which man, if either, is the protagonist, and why. Support your thesis with evidence and quotations from the play.

2- Model: *Julius Caesar* and MLA Format Model

Prompt: Rewrite Mark Antony's entire funeral oration (Act 3, Scene 2) in modern English. Do your best to choose vivid, specific, contemporary language, and be sure to maintain the irony, drama, and pacing of the original. How does modern language change the sound and feeling of the scene? Read the speech aloud, using Marlon Brando's performance in the 1953 movie as a model for dramatic inflection. If you cannot view the movie, use the version at the link in the Video section of the Context Resources.

Turn in the draft at the end of the week, so your writing mentor can evaluate it using the Content standards (Ideas/Concepts and Organization) on the rubric.

Week 4

Use the feedback on the rubric, along with the writing mentor's comments, to revise your paper. Before turning in the final draft, be sure you have addressed any issues marked on the evaluation rubric, and verify that the thesis is clear and your essay is well-organized. Use your writer's handbook to check grammar or punctuation so that your essay will be free from mechanical errors. Turn in the essay at the end of the week so that the writing mentor can use the evaluation rubric in the "How to Evaluate" chapter to check your work.

Module 2.8

Ivanhoe by Sir Walter Scott (1771-1832)

Teach your children poetry; it opens the mind, lends grace to wisdom and makes the heroic virtues hereditary.

—Sir Walter Scott

Focus Text

Ivanhoe by Sir Walter Scott

Honors Texts

Merchant of Venice by William Shakespeare or

Rob Roy by Sir Walter Scott

Literary Period

English Romanticism

Module Focus

In this early example of historical fiction, you will observe how Sir Walter Scott uses heroic adventures, anchored in real events, to illustrate chivalry and nobility in action. By showing virtue, vice, and their consequences in a fictional setting, Scott was able to effectively and memorably convey truth through story, as Aesop did in his fables and Christ did in the parables recorded in scripture.

Introduction

Ivanhoe is a historical novel set in 1194, 128 years after the Norman Conquest and shortly after the end of the Third Crusade. This dramatic adventure begins with Saxon hero, Wilfred of Ivanhoe, out of favor with his father for his allegiance to the Norman king, Richard the Lionhearted.

In the process of regaining his father's good will and the hand of the lovely Rowena, Ivanhoe meets many well-known figures, including Robin Hood and his "merry men," Prince John Lackland, the Knights Templar, and others. Although the language is a bit old-fashioned, it is a story well worth reading; not only for its rollicking good tale, but also for its vivid portrayal of this period in history.

Something to think about . . .

The characters of the Jewish moneylender Isaac of York and his daughter Rebecca are two of the most vivid in the story. At the time Sir Walter Scott wrote *Ivanhoe*, there was an increasing consciousness of injustice toward the Jewish people, and an active movement toward lifting unfair legal restrictions on Jews in England (before 1829, Catholics and Jews lacked many of the rights of an emancipated English citizen). Complete equality was not reached until 1890, but books such as *Ivanhoe* are credited with dramatizing the injustice in a way that helped shape public opinion and build support for reform.

Be sure to notice . . .

Gurth the swineherd and Wamba the jester not only provide a bit of comic relief throughout the story, they also offer the reader a look at a socioeconomic level lower than knights and fair ladies usually encountered in books set in the feudal period. Notice their positions in the household, and the amount of power that Cedric, their master, has over them. As the feudal system gradually disappeared in Europe, power shifted. What were some of the historical events that helped bring about change?

Context Resources

The Author's Life

Sir Walter Scott was a tremendously popular author during his lifetime—one of the first authors to have his work read internationally, and he is sometimes credited with the invention of historical fiction. He fell out of favor after the Victorian era, but has regained a measure of popularity. Begin by reading about him in an encyclopedia or in a short biography. If you choose to read this online biography, be sure to read all fourteen short segments.

http://www.walterscott.lib.ed.ac.uk/biography/index.html

Sir Walter Scott is included in the Famous Authors video series produced in 2007. You may be able to obtain it at your library or bookstore. You may also enjoy reading this short, well-written overview of Scott's life.

http://kirjasto.sci.fi/wscott.htm

Poetry

In an anthology of poetry, look for poetry by Sir Walter Scott. You'll find that his poetic subjects are conveyed with a romantic tone similar to that found in his prose. Many of his poems are book-length ballads, and you will find sections of them presented as individual poems. At the website below, read three or more selections.

http://rpo.library.utoronto.ca/poets/scott-sir-walter

Robert Burns was Scotland's most famous poet during his lifetime, and he remains beloved by many. His work is written in a Scottish dialect that can make it difficult to understand, but you will doubtless be familiar enough with the poems below to catch their meaning. You may read as many others from these sites as you would like.

- Auld Lang Syne: http://www.robertburns.org/works/236.shtml
- A Red, Red Rose: http://www.robertburns.org/works/444.shtml

http://www.robertburns.org

http://rpo.library.utoronto.ca/poets/burns-robert

Audio

You may listen to a professional reading of the book on CD or MP3, or you may download the free amateur recording from Librivox.

http://librivox.org/ivanhoe-by-sir-walter-scott

Excellence in Literature: Reading and Writing through the Classics

Music

If you would like to listen to medieval music as you read the novel, visit Ancient.fm, an online radio station dedicated to medieval music. Select whether you'd like to listen in iTunes, via Shockwave, or by another method, then click and listen.

http://www.ancientfm.com

Read about the development of medieval music in an article from the *Online Reference Book for Medieval Studies* (ORB).

http://excellence-in-literature.com/lit-and-comp/e2-resources/
introduction-to-medieval-music-by-cynthia-cyrus

The Ivory Consort is a contemporary musical group dedicated to the authentic performance of medieval music. At the first link below, you can learn a bit about them by reading a review of one of their performances, then watch videos of their live music at the second link. Be sure to notice the interesting instruments they are playing. To hear samples from their most recent CD, click on the cover shown above.

http://clubs.calvin.edu/chimes/article.php?id=544

http://excellence-in-literature.com/excellence-in-lit/lit-and-comp/e2-resources/
ivory-consort-medieval-music-videos

Here is a page of links to clips of a wide variety of early music.

http://earlymusicchicago.org/recordings_audio_clips.htm

Video

The 1952 version of *Ivanhoe* with Elizabeth Taylor as Rebecca and Joan Fontaine as Rowena and the 1982 made-for-TV version are both well reviewed by Decent-Films.com, with a slight edge to the 1982 version. You may choose which, if any, you prefer; both are available on DVD.

Visual Arts

Medieval art forms include tapestry, painting, carving, sculpting, architecture, manuscript illumination, stained glass, ivories, enameling, and murals. Visit a library or book store and look at the DK Eyewitness Book, *Medieval Life,* by Andrew Langley and at an art history book to view a sampling of typical art.

The *Book of Kells* is often referred to as the most beautiful book in the world. Entirely handwritten and illustrated, its pages are heavily ornamented and detailed. You may read about it and see a few images on the Long Island University site. More images are available at Wikipedia if you would like to see them.

http://www2.liu.edu/cwis/cwp/library/sc/kells/kells.htm

Inspired by the illuminated manuscripts of the medieval era, St. John's Abbey and University commissioned calligrapher Donald Jackson to produce a hand-written, hand-illuminated Bible. It is still a work in progress, but you can see many beautiful pages at this website. Click on "See the Bible," then "Explore each volume" to see selections from the seven sections of this masterwork.

http://www.saintjohnsbible.org

The Cupola site offers several galleries of images of medieval architecture.

http://www.cupola.com/html/bldgstru/medieval/medievo1.htm

Historic Context

Read this brief, authoritative history of the Jewish people in the United Kingdom, 1066–present, from the Jewish Virtual Library.

http://www.jewishvirtuallibrary.org/jsource/vjw/England.html

Look at your local library for the Eyewitness book *Knight* by Christopher Gravett, *Castle* by David MacAulay, and *An Illustrated History of the Knights Templar* by James Wasserman. You do not need to read everything in them, but get acquainted with the basic ideas in each book.

Read about the Invasion of England, 1066 (also known as the Norman Conquest, Battle of Hastings, or simply 1066), so that you will understand why the Saxons were hostile to the Normans. Be sure to read both pages of the narrative here:

http://www.eyewitnesstohistory.com/bayeux.htm

Next, watch the story unfold in a four minute animated video of the Bayeux Tapestry. Do not miss this dramatic tale!

http://excellence-in-literature.com/lit-and-comp/e2-resources/animated-bayeux-tapestry-video

You will notice that in the Bayeux Tapestry the story of the conquest is told from the Norman perspective. If you would like to read the English view, I highly recommend David Howarth's book, *1066: The Year of the Conquest*. It's a completely different view, and the story is very well told.

Use your encyclopedia to read about the Knights Templar, the Normans, the Saxons, and the Battle of Hastings.

Names

It is helpful to know that some of the characters occasionally appear under assumed identities.

The hero, Wilfred of Ivanhoe, also appears in the disguise of a Palmer, a person who has completed a pilgrimage to the Holy Land, and as Desdichado, a Spanish name meaning "unfortunate or disinherited knight."

King Richard I, rightful King of England, is also known as Richard the Lion-Hearted or Richard *Coeur de Lion* in French. When he first appears in the story, he has been imprisoned in Austria, and he re-enters England disguised as the Black Knight.

Robin Hood is known both as Locksley and as Diccon Bend-the-Bow.

Places to Go

If you live near New York City, try to schedule a trip to The Cloisters, an atmospheric branch of The Metropolitan Museum assembled from authentically ancient architectural elements. It contains many interesting medieval objects, including the famed unicorn tapestries.

http://www.metmuseum.org/cloisters

Visit the original Bayeux Tapestry in the charming town of Bayeux in Normandy, France, or the Victorian reproduction in Reading, England. The French museum has the original medieval tapestry, along with related artifacts, and the English museum houses a replica embroidered during the Victorian era (they had to tell the story their way!). I have been to the French museum, and it is well worth a trip if you are in the area. You can even purchase embroidery kits in the gift shop so that you can replicate a bit of the tapestry for yourself.

http://www.tapisserie-bayeux.fr

View the entire English tapestry here:

http://www.bayeuxtapestry.org.uk

Assignment Schedule

Week 1

Begin reading the context resources and the novel. Be sure to notice the epigraphs that introduce each chapter's theme, and as you read, consider how well each epigraph sets the stage for its chapter. Follow the model in the Formats and Models chapter to write an Author Profile. Be sure to refer to your writer's handbook if you have questions about grammar, structure, or style.

Week 2

Finish the readings, and write an approach paper on *Ivanhoe*, using the instructions and samples in the Formats and Models chapter. In addition to the context links I have provided, you may use other resources such as your encyclopedia, the library, and quality Internet resources to help you complete this assignment.

Week 3

Begin drafting a 600-word paper on one of the topics below. I recommend that you follow the writing process outlined in the "How to Write an Essay" chapter, consulting the models in the Formats and Models chapter and your writer's handbook as needed.

1- Model: Literary Analysis Essay and MLA Format Model

Prompt: Consider the effect of divisions in *Ivanhoe*. The Normans are divided from the Saxons, Ivanhoe is separated from his father and Rowena, and Gentiles are separated from Jews. How does Scott use the events of the book to try and resolve these divisions? In what ways is he successful or not successful, and what effect does this have on the satisfactory resolution of the plot?

2- Model: MLA Format Model

Prompt: Disguise is a significant factor in the plot of Ivanhoe. The characters who appear in disguise include Ivanhoe, Richard, Wamba, and Cedric. What is the purpose and meaning of the theme of disguise in the overall novel? What purpose does Scott accomplish by having his characters hide their identities?

Turn in the draft at the end of the week, so your writing mentor can evaluate it using the Content standards (Ideas/Concepts and Organization) on the rubric.

Week 4

Use the feedback on the rubric, along with the writing mentor's comments, to revise your paper. Before turning in the final draft, be sure you have addressed any issues marked on the evaluation rubric, and verify that the thesis is clear and your essay is well-organized. Use your writer's handbook to check grammar or punctuation so that your essay will be free from mechanical errors. Turn in the essay at the end of the week so that the writing mentor can use the evaluation rubric in the "How to Evaluate" chapter to check your work.

Module 2.9

The Importance of Being Earnest by Oscar Wilde (1854-1900)

We are the zanies of sorrow. We are clowns whose hearts are broken.

—Oscar Wilde

Focus Text

The Importance of Being Earnest: A Trivial Comedy for Serious People by Oscar Wilde (1854-1900)

The complete text of *The Importance of Being Earnest* is available as an individual book, or in the *Norton Anthology of English Literature* (9th edition, Vol. 2). You may find it in earlier editions of the Norton Anthology as well.

Honors Text

Kim by Rudyard Kipling (1865–1936)

This tale illustrates Victorian fascination with the exotic and offers another look at colonialism and European Empire-building (as previously studied in *Heart of Darkness*). It is a vivid and fascinating story, graphically conveying the atmosphere and attitudes of the era. You may read a bit about Kipling and his work at this Finnish site:

http://kirjasto.sci.fi/kipling.htm

Literary Period

Romantic/Victorian

Excellence in Literature: Reading and Writing through the Classics

Module Focus

You will learn about the conventions of late Victorian farce, and see how social or political messages can be conveyed through absurdity. You will also observe the dramatic shift in mood and tone from Wilde's *The Importance of Being Earnest* to his later *De Profundis*.

Introduction

The Importance of Being Earnest is a humorous drama set in late Victorian England. The characters in this social farce maintain fictitious identities in order to juggle the social obligations of city and country, and this deceit results in considerable awkwardness. As in most British comedy, the dialogue and action moves quickly, so you may have to read or watch it more than once. Wilde's witty dialogue along with his pointed satire of some of the absurdities of late Victorian society has made this an enduringly popular play.

Something to think about . . .

Under the humor of this farce runs a serious critique of Victorian hypocrisy. Like the Pharisees of Biblical times, the Victorians were sometimes to perceived to be punctiliously following outward rules of conduct while being inwardly corrupt. Unfortunately, Oscar Wilde's worldview led him to believe that it was the conventional rules of conduct that were to blame for the hypocrisy, and he never realized that the problem originated in the unsurrendered hearts of individuals (you may want to think about Titus 1:15 as a possible reason for this). Despite this worldview, he manages to convey the truth about the ugliness of hypocrisy and the damage that can result when living a life of deception.

A particularly vivid example of hypocrisy is the scene in which a young lady suddenly becomes an attractive and acceptable match for a young man when Lady Bracknell learns that she will be quite wealthy once she is of age. Watch for other example of events which appear funny, but have a serious message. Remember that much of what is said is ironic, and Wilde excelled in the use of puns, so many scenes can be evaluated for what they say as well as what they actually mean.

Be sure to notice . . .

In order to create a successful farce, it is necessary for each actor to play his or her part as though it is perfectly serious. As you watch the play, notice that even the most outrageously absurd scenes are played as though everyone is behaving reasonably.

Context Resources

Readings

The official website of the British monarchy has a good biography of Queen Victoria after whom the Victorian era is named.

http://www.royal.gov.uk/HistoryoftheMonarchy/KingsandQueensoftheUnitedKingdom/TheHanoverians/Victoria.aspx

Here is a site with downloadable copies of all of Oscar Wilde's works.

http://www.oscarwildecollection.com

This brief, satirical series of cartoons describes "How to Finish a Daughter."

http://harpersbazaar.victorian-ebooks.com/Nov2_1867/11-1txt.html

If you enjoy British humor, you may also enjoy the quirky humor of Jerome K. Jerome in *Three Men in a Boat* and P. G. Wodehouse in his Bertie and Jeeves novels. These classics offer a broad glimpse of British life and humor, and you will probably find yourself laughing out loud.

The Author's Life

Oscar Wilde was an intelligent, complex, hardworking man and an immensely gifted writer, but he lived a decadent life and was eventually tried and imprisoned for indecency. His imprisonment and exile affected him deeply, and his life and writings after his release were quite different from what he wrote earlier. Read this brief biography written by his son, Vyvyan Holland, then read Holland's brief biography as well, as it offers more insight into the impact of Wilde's disgrace. You are not required to read any other biographical information about Wilde.

http://www.mr-oscar-wilde.de/biography/introduction.htm

http://www.mr-oscar-wilde.de/about/h/holland_v.htm

Read Wilde's prison letter, *De Profundis* for insight into Wilde's thoughts near the end of his life. This is very important. Do not miss it!

http://excellence-in-literature.com/lit-and-comp/e2-resources/de-profundis-by-oscar-wilde

Wilde is buried in Père Lachaise Cemetery in Paris, and the epitaph on his monument is a verse from *The Ballad of Reading Gaol*:

"And alien tears will fill for him
Pity's long-broken urn,
For his mourners will be outcast men,
And outcasts always mourn."

Poetry

Here are two examples of Oscar Wilde's poetry:

"On The Massacre Of The Christians In Bulgaria":

http://excellence-in-literature.com/lit-and-comp/e2-resources/
on-the-massacre-of-the-christians-in-bulgaria-by-oscar-wilde

"The Ballad Of Reading Gaol" (pronounced "Redding Jail"): This poem was written
after Wilde's imprisonment, and I recommend listening to it, rather than reading it. Here is a link below to an audio reading of "The Ballad of Reading Gaol."
It is not professionally done, so if you can get a better rendition at your library,
you may want to do so. The description contains incorrect information about
his cause of death, so feel free to ignore it.

http://librivox.org/the-ballad-of-reading-gaol-by-oscar-wilde-jg

Light verse was very popular during the Victorian era, and I think you will enjoy
samples from two of the most popular poets. Read each poet's brief biography,
and at least the recommended poem (you may read others too).

Lewis Carroll: "The Walrus and the Carpenter"

(Bio and link to poem): http://www.poets.org/poet.php/prmPID/78

(poem): http://excellence-in-literature.com/lit-and-comp/e2-resources/
the-walrus-and-the-carpenter-by-lewis-carroll

Edward Lear: "The Jumblies"

http://excellence-in-literature.com/lit-and-comp/e2-resources/the-jumblies-by-ed-
ward-lear or

http://www.poets.org/poet.php/prmPID/140

The Victorians could be serious as well, and Kipling's "If . . . " is inspiring.

Rudyard Kipling: "If . . . "

http://excellence-in-literature.com/lit-and-comp/e2-resources/
if-poem-by-rudyard-kipling

Audio

It is better to watch *The Importance of Being Earnest* than to listen to it, if only for the facial expressions of the characters, but if you cannot watch, listening to an audio drama is the next best thing. Here is a link to the free performance if your library does not have a professional recording. I have not listened to it all, so I do not know about the quality of the performers. It will at least give you an idea of what the play is like.

http://librivox.org/the-importance-of-being-earnest-by-oscar-wilde

Here is an audio recording of John Gielgud and Edith Evans doing the scene of Lady Bracknell interrogating John/Ernest Worthing. This includes the famous "handbag" line, as well as the lines, "To lose one parent may be regarded as a misfortune–to lose both seems like carelessness," and other incomparable quips, perfectly delivered. Do not miss this!

http://excellence-in-literature.com/lit-and-comp/e2-resources/john-gielgud-and-
edith-evans-perform-the-handbag-scene-from-wildes-importance-of-being-earnest

Music

Victorian Light Opera was an art form that flourished during Wilde's lifetime. These compositions were similar to musicals of the 20th century. Here are some MIDI or karaoke versions of Victorian and Edwardian light operas.

http://www.halhkmusic.com

Brass bands gained popularity during the Victorian era. The public bandstand, a circular or semicircular structure, usually with open sides, became a popular feature during this era, and is still widely used for public performances in parks and on piers. Dr. Stephen Rhodes of Lipscomb University has written *A History of the Wind Band*, and you can read the interesting chapter on "The British Brass Band" at his website below:

http://www.lipscomb.edu/windbandhistory/RhodesWindBand_07_BritishBrassBand.
htm

Brass bands play both classical selections and pieces written especially for brass band. Some of the most popular current composers include Philip Sparke and T. J. (Tom) Powell, as well as classical composers Ralph (pronounced "Rafe") Vaughan Williams, Edward Elgar, and Gustav Holst who also wrote music for brass bands. In an encyclopedia, read about at least two of these composers and listen to the music clips at the Ralph Vaughan Williams site.

http://www.rvwsociety.com/soundsmps/symphsounds.html

Video

The Importance of Being Ernest was filmed in 1952 with Michael Redgrave as Ernest/John Worthing. Because Wilde wrote this as a drama, it is necessary to see it, with all the player's facial expressions, in order to get the effect he intended. After you hear Lady Bracknell say "handbag," you will probably never again hear the word without thinking of her. You may watch a few clips from this film at the link below.

http://excellence-in-literature.com/lit-and-comp/
e2-resources/1952-film-the-importance-of-being-earnest-clip

Visual Arts

In an art history encyclopedia or at the link below, look at the following works by artists whose works reflect some of the same artistic ideas as the work of Oscar Wilde.

- Henri de Toulouse-Lautrec: Jane Avril Leaving the Moulin Rouge
- Edgar Degas: Place de la Concorde and Ballet Rehearsal, or Portrait of a Woman in Gray and Dancer
- Gustav Klimt: Adele Bloch-Bauer I
- Alphonse Mucha: Poster of Maude Adams as Joan of Arc, or The Four Seasons: Spring

http://excellence-in-literature.com/lit-and-comp/e2-resources/victorian-art

Historic Context

If you have a *Norton Anthology of British Literature*, read the introduction to the Victorian era. Visit these two pages at the Norton website for additional information:

http://www.wwnorton.com/college/english/nael/victorian/welcome.htm

http://www.wwnorton.com/college/english/nael/victorian/review/mconnections.htm

Visit the British Library website for an excellent overview of the Victorian era. Click on each of the links on this page and read the information presented.

http://www.bl.uk/learning/histcitizen/victorians/victorianhome.html

The British Library also offers a fascinating virtual timeline. Scroll over until you reach the card decks for the 19th century, then click on them to learn more about the Victorian era. When you click on individual cards, they will flip over, displaying more information.

http://www.bl.uk/learning/timeline/index.html

Assignment Schedule

Week 1

Read and watch *The Importance of Being Earnest*, and read *De Profundis* and the context resources about the author's life. Follow the model in the Formats and Models chapter to write an Author Profile. Be sure to refer to your writer's handbook if you have questions about grammar, structure, or style.

Week 2

Retell *The Importance of Being Earnest* as a short story. Be sure to include vivid detail, suspense, and humor, just as Wilde did. Make it at least 300 words long, or as long as necessary to tell a good story. In addition to the context links I have provided, you may use other resources such as your encyclopedia, the library, and quality Internet resources to complete this assignment.

Week 3

Begin drafting a 600-word paper on one of the topics below. I recommend that you follow the writing process outlined in the "How to Write an Essay" chapter, consulting the models in the Formats and Models chapter and your writer's handbook as needed.

1- Model: Literary Analysis Essay and MLA Format Model

Prompt: Discuss the pun in the title of the book. Who, if anyone, is being earnest in this play? Does it seem that Gwendolen and Cecily prefer having husbands named Ernest or having earnest husbands? What does this say about the Victorian values?

2- MLA Format Model

Prompt: Some critics have stated that in *The Importance of Being Earnest* Wilde is primarily concerned with pointing out the difference between conventional and actual manners and morality in Victorian society. Use specific examples to illustrate what you believe Wilde is saying that Victorians practice in one or two of the following areas: marriage and courtship, class structure, money and property, or attitudes towards illness and death, and the difference between what they practice and what they say. Compare and contrast their speech with their actions, and evaluate how closely they adhere to principles of honesty, morality, and wholesome living, and whether or not Wilde's portrayal seems true to reality.

For additional help, use your writer's handbook or refer to the "How to Write a Compare/Contrast Essay " article at the first URL below, and see a model at the second URL:

http://excellence-in-literature.com/resources-for-teaching/
how-to-write-a-compare-contrast-essay

http://excellence-in-literature.com/resources-for-teaching/
sample-compare-contrast-essay

Turn in the draft at the end of the week, so your writing mentor can evaluate it using the Content standards (Ideas/Concepts and Organization) on the rubric.

Week 4

Use the feedback on the rubric, along with the writing mentor's comments, to revise your paper. Before turning in the final draft, be sure you have addressed any issues marked on the evaluation rubric, and verify that the thesis is clear and your essay is well-organized. Use your writer's handbook to check grammar or punctuation so that your essay will be free from mechanical errors. Turn in the essay at the end of the week so that the writing mentor can use the evaluation rubric in the "How to Evaluate" chapter to check your work.

Honors

Excellence is doing ordinary things extraordinarily well.

—John W. Gardner

Key components of the Honors Option (in addition to regular assignments related to the focus text) include reading, writing, and a final exam. The reading is the most time-consuming element, as it is the foundation for both the writing assignment and the final exam. Be sure to create a schedule that makes it manageable:

- Extra reading with an approach paper for each book
- One 6- to 10-page research paper (depending on student's grade level)
- CLEP test for some levels

Extra Reading

Extra reading for honors students will be listed on the syllabus. Some items will be additional works by authors we are studying; other items will be context works that will help to round out knowledge of each literary period or understanding of the theme. Honors reading may be done during or between semesters and should be recorded in the reading log.

Approach Papers

For one full-length honors text per module, the student should complete an approach paper. If more than one honors text is suggested, the student may choose which to read (though it can be beneficial to read all of them) and which to use as the subject for the approach paper. It is not necessary to write more than one honors approach paper per module.

Research Paper

This 6- to 10-page paper, due two weeks after the end of the spring semester, will be a research paper on your choice of the authors you have studied this year. The paper will be presented in MLA format (http://owl.english.purdue.edu/owl/resource/747/01/) and will include a Works Cited page, with a minimum of four resources. Up to two of the resources may be Internet sources chosen in accordance with accepted academic standards. For detailed instructions on the process of researching, writing, and documenting a research paper, you will need to consult your writing handbook.

Suggestions for the Author Research Paper

A research paper has been described as a thoughtful inquiry into a topic you find interesting. You will find detailed instructions in most writer's handbooks for how to do research, keep track of sources, list citations, format your research paper, and so forth. Once you have decided on the author who will be the focus of your Honors paper, here are things you may want to include:

- overview of the author's life
- people, groups, and events that influenced the author's life and writing
- overview of the author's body of work and his or her reputation among peers and in the general public
- analysis of one or more of the author's best- or least-known works
- how the author's work has influenced later writers or a genre of literature

CLEP Test

The comprehensive final exam, which will be taken at the end of the school year, will be the British Literature CLEP. This ninety-minute, multiple-choice, computer-based exam can be taken by appointment at a local college or community college. Many colleges and universities grant advanced placement and/or college credit (usually six credits) for a passing score on this exam, so it is well worth the effort. (I earned forty-five credits toward my B.A. by taking exams on subjects I had studied on my own.) You may learn more about CLEP exams at www.CollegeBoard.com.

Excellence in Literature: Assignment Checklist

Student: **School Year:**

Grade: **English II: Literature and Composition**

	Week 1		Week 2		Week 3		Week 4	
	Assignment	Date	Assignment	Date	Assignment	Date	Assignment	Date
Module 2.1- DeFoe								
Module 2.2- Thoreau								
Module 2.3- Dumas								
Module 2.4- Conrad								
Module 2.5- Lewis								
Module 2.6- Cather								
Module 2.7- Shakespeare								
Module 2.8- Scott								
Module 2.9- Wilde								

For each module, list the assignment and the date due or completed (your choice).

Sample Listing

Module #- Example	Author profile	01/07	Approach paper	01/14	750-word essay draft	01/21	Final draft of essay	01/28

Excellence in Literature: Student Evaluation Summary

Student: **School Year:**

Letter Grade: **English II: Literature and Composition**

	Ideas/ Concepts	Organi- zation	Voice	Word Choice	Sentence Fluency	Mechanics	Presen- tation	Total
Module 2.1- DeFoe								
Module 2.2- Thoreau								
Module 2.3- Dumas								
Module 2.4- Conrad								
Module 2.5- Lewis								
Module 2.6- Cather								
Module 2.7- Shakespeare								
Module 2.8- Scott								
Module 2.9- Wilde								
Total								
Average								

Class Description

Literature and Composition is a college-preparatory literature and composition course. Focus works, including novels, short stories, poems, and drama have been selected for literary quality and for their place in the historic development of literature.

Context readings provide background information about the author, and historic, literary, and artistic context of the focus work. Students will practice the skills of close literary analysis through essays, approach papers, and other writing.

Course Objectives

By the end of the course, students will:

- Understand the process of writing, including the use of tools such as a writer's handbook, dictionary, and thesaurus.
- Have specific understanding of selected representative texts by major authors of the periods studied.
- Have a general understanding of the historical and cultural contexts of the works.
- Be able to analyze literary texts and present thoughtfully developed ideas in writing.
- Demonstrate competence in essay organization, style, and mechanics.
- Demonstrate competence in the MLA style of source documentation.

Evaluations

Student writing is evaluated using the Excellence in Writing evaluation rubric. Each paper is analyzed and evaluated in the following seven areas: Ideas and Concepts, Organization, Voice, Word Choice, Sentence Fluency, Mechanics, and Presentation. Course grade is based upon essays (65%), shorter assignments (15%), vocabulary development (10%), and studentship (10%).

Comments

Formats and Models

Example is the school of mankind, and they will learn at no other.

—Edmund Burke

There is a long and honorable tradition of using models or samples to learn to write well. The formats and models are you find here will help you understand the elements of each kind of assignment you will do. Each basic type of paper practiced in EIL is presented with a "Format"—instructions for what each paper should contain—plus a "Model"—a student-written sample of what a completed paper might look like. These models have been used with the permission of some of my former students and are examples of what each type of assignment should contain when it is turned in.

The final paper in this section is a general model of an essay written in MLA format with examples of how to integrate and format quotations of prose or poetry. This model will be useful for all your Week 3 writing assignments.

In every assignment, please use MLA format (see the final model in this section, titled "MLA Format Model"). Remember to put your name, the date, the class name, and the module number and focus text title in the top left corner of each assignment you turn in. For essays or stories, also copy the assignment prompt just below this information so that you will have it handy as you are writing, and your evaluator will know exactly what question you are answering.

Note to Parents About the Model Papers

When you look at these papers, please do not panic. They are the work of some of my best students over the years, and they offer a look at what is possible, not necessarily what is routinely expected. If your student is not producing work of this caliber yet, be patient. With each completed assignment you will see growth and improvement, and that incremental growth is what you will build on. You do not have to start at the top to have good results; you just need to climb steadily!

↶

Approach Paper Format

One of my favorite tools for literary analysis is the approach paper. Although "approach paper" may seem to be an odd name for an analytical assignment, it makes sense when you realize that the exercise of writing each section of the approach paper helps to guide your thinking as you approach the essay assignment.

An approach paper consists of several sections:

I. **MLA-style heading** with your name, date, class, and name of the work you will be analyzing. (See sample for proper format.)

II. **Summary Paragraph:** A three- or four-sentence paragraph that summarizes the book or other work in as much descriptive detail as possible. Each of the sentences in your summary must begin in a different way, and sentences should be varied in length and full of interesting detail. Your writing handbook will provide specific help in sentence formatting and styling, plus guidance for correcting unclear or incomplete sentences. The summary is sometimes the most difficult section of the approach paper to write because it takes time to condense the events of the novel/play into just a few well-written sentences!

III. **Character Descriptions:** Choose and list three or four main characters in the work you are studying. In just four or five adjectives, vividly describe the character. This is a good time to use unique vocabulary words and to check the dictionary and thesaurus for ideas. Descriptive words may be used only once per approach paper, so if you use a word to describe one character, you may not use the same word to describe another character.

IV. **Discussion/Essay Questions:** Write three questions about the novel, poem, play, or essay. These questions should be thought-provoking and will almost always take more than one line to type because they ask readers to combine more than one idea. They must not be questions of fact, but of interpretation, just like the questions that are provided for your essay assignments. The act of writing this type of question helps you to think more insightfully about the characters in relationship to one another and to the setting, the author's style and intention, and the voice and reliability of the narrator. When you think seriously about these issues, you begin to approach an understanding of the text.

V. **Key Passage**: Choose the passage you feel is the most important passage in the work. This may be a brief paragraph, or it may be an entire page or more. Type it up word-for-word in the approach paper. Be sure to identify the speakers if the passage includes dialogue.

VI. **Key Passage Explanation**: In a fully developed paragraph, explain why your chosen passage is important to understanding the focus text. In your explanation make sure you integrate quotes (actual words or phrases) from the key passage to strengthen your explanation, using proper MLA format as demonstrated in your handbook or in the sample essay in this guide. Often, your chosen key passage will offer clues to the novel/play's themes. Explain any mentioned or inferred themes connected to the key passage.

⌒

Approach Paper Model

Student's Name

Date

English V: Instructor's Name

Don Quixote Approach Paper

Summary:

    Don Quixote by Miguel de Cervantes is the classic tale of a Spanish madman named Don Quixote, who decides to become a knight. Along with his devoted squire Sancho Panza, Don Quixote forces himself and others into undesirable adventures throughout the Spanish nation of Castille. But Don Quixote also finds that the world does not desire a return to the old world of chivalry, for he is scorned at every turn for his desire to revive a long-lost golden age of Europe. On two different occasions, in fact, a bachelor named Sansón Carrasco (disguised as a knight-errant) tries to defeat the deluded knight in jousts, attempting to order him to return to his hometown in La Mancha. On the second attempt, Sansón defeats Don Quixote, and grants him life under the condition that he return to his home and forsake the order of knight-errantry. After Don Quixote returns home, he regains his sanity and declares, "I now abhor all profane stories of knight-errantry."

Characters

- Sancho Panza: gullible, subservient, opportunistic, acquisitive
- Don Quixote: quixotic*, idealistic, chimerical, fatuous, psychotic
- Sansón Carrasco: covetous, arrogant, avaricious, pugnacious

Discussion Questions

- The characters in *Don Quixote* make numerous references to Miguel de Cervantes himself, as though the author were a contemporary of the characters. How is the author's opinion about himself portrayed in the book? What attributes of Cervantes' own life and philosophy are expressed within the characters?
- Much of the parody in *Don Quixote* is affected by the unusual combination between knight-errantry and sixteenth-century life. How do the civilizations of Amadis of Gaul and King Arthur of England differ from Don Quixote's world?
- Cervantes makes many references to the relationship between Moors and Christians in sixteenth-century Spain. Has the relationship changed since the age when the Moors were driven out of Spain? If so, how?

Key Passage, from Chapter XV of Book II, p. 627

In his first joust with Sansón Carrasco, Don Quixote emerges victorious from battle and elated with joy over his triumph. Afterward, the following passage ensues:

> Carrasco undertook the task [to defeat Don Quixote in a joust], and Tomé Cecial, Sancho's comrade and neighbor, a merry, scatterbrained fellow, offered his services as squire. Sansón armed himself as has been described and Tomé Cecial, to avoid being recognized by his comrade when they met, fitted on over his natural nose the false one already mentioned. And so they followed the same road as Don Quixote and very nearly reached him in time to be present at the adventure of the cart of Death, and at last they met in the wood, where everything that the extraordinary fancies of Don Quixote, who took it into his head that the bachelor was not the bachelor, Master Bachelor licentiate, because he did not find nests where he expected to find birds. Tomé Cecial, seeing how badly their plans had turned out and what a wretched end their expedition had come to, said to the bachelor: "For sure, Master Sansón Carrasco, we've met with our deserts. It is easy to plan and start an enterprise, but most times it

is hard to get out of it safe and sound. Don Quixote is mad, and we are sane, but he comes off safe and in high spirits, while you, master, are left drubbed and downcast. Tell us, now, who is the greater madman, he who is so because he cannot help it, or he who is so of his own free will?"

Key Passage Explanation:

This passage offers a panoramic view of the whole paradox of Don Quixote. Don Quixote is mad, but the sane madness of his opponents is even worse, for in their depravity they are mad of their "own free will." We see in this passage that everyone is a sort of villain in this book. Don Quixote meets with his own hardships, but as Tomé Cecial points out, "We've met with our own deserts [deserved punishments]." Cervantes does not advocate the false chivalry promulgated in the books of knight-errantry, but neither does he support its alternative. By ridiculing both extremes, Cervantes tacitly expresses his desire for a balance.

~

Historical Approach Paper Format

Event or Era

Place

Time

Event Summary

Write an interesting one-paragraph summary of the period or event.

Key Players

Choose 3–4 key people involved in the event, and list 4–5 vividly descriptive words for each person. Words may not be used to describe more than one character.

Discussion Questions

Think carefully about the event, and write three analytical discussion questions.

Turning Point

Choose an event that seems to mark a significant turning point or climax in the period or event, and write a one-paragraph description.

Why do you believe this was a significant turning point? What happened afterward? Write a fully developed paragraph explaining your choice. Support your argument with quotes from the text or other sources, if appropriate.

∽

Historical Approach Paper Model

Student's Name

Date

English I: Instructor's Name

Event: Russian Revolution

Place: Russia

Time: 1917

Event/Era Summary

The Russian Revolution was not a single event in which Tsar Nicholas II was defeated and removed from power, but a broad expression of two events, the February Revolution and the October Revolution. Leading up to the February Revolution, Russia experienced turmoil and political conflict over issues such as the country's economic condition and its prevailing failure in World War I. Conditions in Russia continued to worsen until a festival in one of Russia's prominent cities turned into a large protest, inducing Nicholas II to order a military intervention which proved futile, as much of his military was no longer loyal. This event caused Nicholas II to resign the position of tsar to his brother, Michael Alexandrovich, who was not willing to serve without election. Without anyone to fill the position, Russia had no other choice than to set up a temporary government, eventually headed by Alexander Kerensky. Another important character, Vladimir Lenin, plays a significant role in the October Revolution as a member of the communist revolution with a plan to overthrow the current government. Lenin's plan worked to perfection as military guards laid down their arms immediately without resistance. Alexander Kerensky soon fled the palace and the new government, led by Lenin, took effect.

Key Players

- Tsar Nicholas II: obstinate, neglectful, destructive, intelligent
- Vladimir Lenin: persuasive, radical, visionary, rebellious
- Alexander Kerensky: popular, successful, convincing, renowned

Discussion Questions

I.   Though it may have been due to his lack of political education, Nicholas II made many mistakes as a leader. What measures could he have taken in an attempt to avoid the widespread upheaval that occurred?

II.   Why was Vladimir Lenin so successful in spreading the principles of Marxism? Did the people find hope in his ideas when it seemed as if there was no hope?

III. How did conditions change in Russia after the Revolution of 1917? In what ways did relations with other countries change?

Turning Point

Forced by the growing pressure to turn the economic momentum around and by overall unpopularity, Tsar Nicholas II stepped out of office. He gave his leadership role to his younger brother; however, he would not accept it without the vote of the people. Out of necessity the Russian Provisional Government was assembled in Petrograd to form some type of leadership.

Turing Point Explanation

The time of the resignation of Tsar Nicholas II is the first radical change of the Russian Revolution, but it also marks the end of tsarist rule in Russia. This created a need for a political change to sustain the government, leading into the Russian Provisional Government. Although this occurred during the February Revolution, these events allowed the happenings of the October Revolution to take place, thus completing the entire Revolution of 1917. This time period is a turning point because it started the transformation and provided an outlet for the following events to occur. Without these events it would have been extremely difficult for Lenin and his followers to procure leadership.

Author Profile Format

For each focus work it is important to complete an Author Profile. If you cannot find the recommended biography in your local library, feel free to substitute any short biography that you find. I suggest using biographies found in the middle-grade or young adult sections of the library, as they usually provide an adequate introduction to the author's life without dwelling unnecessarily on the less savory bits.

Name (including pseudonyms if any)

Birth Date   **Place**

Death Date   **Place**

Best-Known Works

Include three or more of the author's best or best-known works.

Brief Biography

- How does this author use his or her personal experiences in his or her work?
- What current events or public figures affected the author's life and writing?
- How do the places in the author's life show up in his or her writing?

Author Profile Model

Name: Washington Irving (pseudonyms include Dietrich Knickerbocker, Jonathan Oldstyle, and Geoffrey Crayon)

Birth Date: April 3, 1783   **Place:** Manhattan, NYC, NY

Death Date: November 28, 1859   **Place:** Sunnyside, Irvington, NY

Best-Known Works

- *The Legend of Sleepy Hollow, Rip Van Winkle, The Sketchbook of Geoffrey Crayon, The Life of George Washington, Knickerbocker's History of New York*

Brief Biography

Washington Irving used his experiences living in both Europe and America to write humorous and meditative stories popular in both the new and old worlds. Irving's life and work were influenced by the events of the Revolutionary War and the War of 1812, and he was also profoundly influenced by other writers (both European and American) of his time. His favorite childhood stories involved voyages to far-off lands. The places of Irving's life show up extensively in his writing. He wrote of England, America, and even lived in Tarrytown, New York, where he set *The Legend of Sleepy Hollow*.

⌒

Literature Summary Format

Novel or Story Title: Write the story's full title and subtitle, if any, here.

Author: Write the author's full name and pseudonym, if any.

Theme: What is the main idea that the author wants to convey? The theme is the big idea illustrated by the story's plot and characters. This can often be expressed in a proverb or phrase such as "honesty is the best policy" or "love never fails."

Characterization: WHO is the story about, and what are they like? How does the author show you this?

Plot: WHAT happens in the story?

Setting: WHEN and WHERE does the story take place?

Style: HOW does the author create a mood and tell the story?

⌒

Literature Summary Model

Novel or Story Title: "The Secret Life of Walter Mitty"

Author: James Thurber

Theme

"The Secret Life of Walter Mitty" explores the desire of every human being to be smarter, braver, and more important, and what happens when this fantasy world becomes an addiction more real than reality itself.

Characterization

Walter Mitty is humanity taken to an extreme. He is a daydreamer, imagining he is a Navy pilot flying through the most devastating hurricane in history when he is just driving his wife to her hair appointment, or envisioning himself as a world-renowned surgeon when he drives past a hospital. You also get the feeling that Walter may be aging and not "all there."

Plot

"The Secret Life of Walter Mitty" chronicles a day in Mitty's life and his struggles to complete his daily routine instead of slipping into his fantasy world.

Setting

The setting of 1940s England has very little effect on the story, except that certain buildings Mitty passes do occasionally prompt certain daydreams.

Style

The story is handled with a rather straightforward, simple style that changes for each daydream. For example, when he imagines himself as a combat pilot, the characters speak with an efficient, clipped style, using only as many words as are necessary.

Literary Analysis Model

This model corresponds with the instructions found in the chapters on "How to Read a Book" and "How to Write an Essay." You will find this model helpful for most of the essays assigned throughout the curriculum. Additional models can be found in the Excellence in Literature *Handbook for Writers*.

Student Name

Date

Class Name

Module # and Focus Text Title

Prompt

Pride and Prejudice was originally titled *First Impressions*. Consider both titles in relation to the characters of Elizabeth, Darcy, and Mr. Wickham, as well as to Austen's depiction of social class. What are the roles of pride, prejudice, and first impressions in the development of relationships among these characters and their social circles? What does Austen seem to suggest about pride, prejudice, and first impressions? Be sure to note Austen's use of irony, and provide specific textual support for your thesis.

The Defects of Human Nature

Life in the early 1800s revolved primarily around the social aspects of life. Social conventions ruled the actions of young ladies and their mothers, guided their brothers in selecting a spouse, and even dictated with whom their families were permitted to associate. Jane Austen gently ridicules the rigid structure of her society's rules and regimens in her novel *Pride and Prejudice*. Through her ironic situations and comical views of life, she attempts to reveal some of society's faults and offer alternatives for the faulty tendencies of human nature.

Pride was an integral part of the nineteenth-century culture. At the very foundation of the separations between social classes, pride enabled entire families to choose not to associate with each other so as not to damage their own social reputations. Mr. Darcy, "a fine figure of a man" with "ten thousand [pounds] a year" (16), embodied this pride admirably. During the first ball he attended in Hertfordshire, his air of superiority proved that he was assuredly aware that his fortune was much larger than anyone's in the room and that his social status was accordingly higher. His reclusive nature and manners also added to the aura of pride which enveloped him.

Although his neighbors were gentlemen and gentlemen's daughters, Mr. Darcy believed that his income and social standing in London set him above the residents of Hertfordshire. Indeed, later he acknowledged that his parents "almost taught [him] to be selfish and overbearing—to care for none beyond [his] own family circle, to think meanly of all the rest of the world, to wish at least to think meanly of their sense and worth compared with [his] own" (274).

Mr. Darcy further displayed the pride which was so deeply ingrained in him when he bungled his first proposal to Elizabeth Bennet. Although he began acceptably with expressions of his love, "he was not more eloquent on the subject of tenderness than of pride" (149). The descriptions of his admiration soon turned to illustrations of the obstacles he overcame to stand before her and propose. Despite his intended purpose to depict the depth of his emotion, his expressions of "his sense of her inferiority … of the family obstacles which judgment had always opposed to inclination" (149) only served to anger and insult Elizabeth. Mr. Darcy's pride prevented him from understanding that the differences in social standing were evident to Elizabeth and that she would not be flattered by his explanations.

Although Elizabeth was not proud in the same manner as Mr. Darcy, she was not immune to human faults. Elizabeth's flaw was expressed in the more socially acceptable form of prejudice. Elizabeth discovered the danger of relying on first impressions as her relationships with Mr. Darcy developed. Mr. Darcy's actions at their first meeting prompted her to accept her community's harsh opinion of him as her own. Without making the effort to get to know Mr. Darcy, Elizabeth fixed her own views about his character and held "no very cordial feelings towards him" (17).

Elizabeth then repeated her mistake of allowing her impressions to turn into prejudice when she met Mr. Wickham. "… Struck with [Mr. Wickham's] air" (63) she formed her acquaintance with an inclination to approve of his actions. This inclination caused her to believe Mr. Wickham explicitly when he fabricated tales about Mr. Darcy. It reached to the extent that her friend felt the need to advise her not to "allow her fancy for Wickham to make her appear unpleasant in the eyes of a man of ten times his consequence" (77).

Ironically, Elizabeth did not begin to alter her prejudices until she accused Mr. Darcy of causing Mr. Wickham's "misfortune" (150). Mr. Darcy's account of the matters forced her to reverse her opinions about him and Mr. Wickham. "Every lingering struggle in [Mr. Wickham's] favor grew fainter and fainter" (161) as she recognized his indecent behavior and consequently scolded herself for not identifying them sooner. This discovery of the true character of these gentlemen was humiliating to Elizabeth as she had "prided [herself] on [her] discernment" (162). However painful this lesson may have been, Elizabeth benefited from it by gaining insight into the hazards of prejudice.

Although Jane Austen first titled her novel *First Impressions*, her final choice of *Pride and Prejudice* seems to fit her analysis of human behavior more suitably. Her humorous novel prodded her contemporaries to formulate their own opinions and not to rely on society's poor abilities or their own preconceived notions about themselves. It forced their descendants to confront their own human nature and face their personal defects.

∽

Sample Poetry Analysis Model

Student Name

Date

Class Name

Module # and Focus Text Title

Prompt: Make a close reading of "God's Grandeur" or "The Windhover" by Gerard Manley Hopkins. Make sure you show how the images and figurative language in the poem complement one another. Show also how he uses sound, including consonance, assonance, and rhyme in constructing his poetic argument. Consider also how he develops his poetic argument from the beginning to the end of his poem.

Inspired by a Falcon

In "The Windhover," Gerard Manley Hopkins talks about watching a kestrel, a small falcon which hovers in the air. Dedicated to Christ, this poem celebrates the majesty, beauty, and power of one of God's creations. Hopkins describes the kestrel's flight, hovering, and dive, as well as his reaction to this display of strength. He is clearly awed, for "[his] heart …Stirred for a bird" (7–8).

Hopkins uses figurative language and imagery throughout "The Windhover." The title itself conveys the image of the kestrel hovering in the wind. In addition, the sounds of the poem correspond with its action.

In the first stanza Hopkins describes the kestrel's steady flying and gliding, as well as the poet's own admiration. The poem begins with "I caught this morning morning's minion, king- / dom of daylight's dauphin, dapple-dawn-drawn Falcon," (1–2).

The word "caught" is used figuratively, as in seen. The word "minion" means darling, and "Dauphin" is the title for the prince who is the heir to the French throne; Hopkins is acknowledging that the kestrel is the darling and ruler of the daylight. He admires "the achieve of, the mastery of the thing!" (7–8), as the kestrel flies uninhibited, master of flying and the air. Hopkins's use of the words "riding" (2) and "striding" (3) help us to see the image of the kestrel flying through the air. In addition, these words give us a sense of the kestrel moving smoothly with a sense of rhythm, which meshes well with his later image of skating. The kestrel glides or hovers through the air, just "As a skate's heel sweeps smooth on a bow-bend" (6).

This stanza has a rhythm that swings along, heightened by alliteration, assonance, and consonance, as in "dapple-dawn-drawn[.]" Later in the stanza Hopkins uses alliteration again to produce a smooth sound that imitates gliding. In addition, the way every line rhymes (they all end with "-ing") also emphasizes rhythm.

In the next stanza Hopkins is talking about the kestrel flying up and then diving down. He uses figurative language to convey the action. "Brute beauty and valour and act, oh, air, pride, plume, here / Buckle! AND the fire that breaks from thee" (9–10). Hopkins describes the kestrel by its attributes, and the combined effect is an impression of soaring and climbing. The bird is not "valour and act ... air, pride, plume," but it and its flight embody those ideas. "Buckle!" and its possible meanings are a one-word summary of what is happening: to get ready, to make fast, to fall through. The poem builds up speed and dives with the windhover. Hopkins uses lots of different consonants and vowels to create a jumbled sound of words climbing upon one another, building up to "Buckle!" just as the kestrel climbs up and then dives. The "fire that breaks from [the kestrel]" refers to the way the kestrel's wings flash open, revealing a reddish-brown color, as the bird nears the ground. Later in the stanza Hopkins refers to the windhover as a "chevalier" (11), which conveys the idea of nobility and strength and "valour" (9). A knight gallops across the countryside; the kestrel hovers and dives in the sky.

In the last stanza the poem flies swiftly and easily to the ground with the bird. This stanza is more quiet; Hopkins uses soft-sounding vowels and consonants. "Sheer plod make plough down sillion / Shine" (12–13) has smooth consonants that move steadily forward just like a plow. Hopkins compares this to the way the kestrel plows through the air. Matching with the earlier figurative language of fire, Hopkins presents an image of "blue-bleak embers, ah my dear, [that] / Fall, gall themselves, and gash gold-vermilion." The embers are falling, opening, and glowing. This helps us to see the image of the kestrel diving through the sky and flashing open his reddish-brown wings when he nears the ground, just as the embers "gash gold-vermilion." In the last line, "Fall, gall themselves, and gash gold-vermilion" (14), even though the g's are hard, the vowel sounds; particularly the use of ah (definitely an example of assonance), soften the line.

Throughout "The Windhover," Hopkins's awe is evident in his enthusiastic description. He conveys his message with words and sounds that echo and emphasize his story, making it a poem of both visual images and oral expression. He uses this method to involve and engage the reader in his experience. Hopkins's soaring poetry shares his awe of the kestrel and its Creator with the reader.

MLA Format Model

Use these format guidelines for all assignments.

Your Name

Date

Class Name

Module # and Focus Text Title

For an EIL essay, please add the writing prompt at this point.

Making Your Essay Look Good:

The Basics of MLA Format

In the upper right-hand corner of each page, beginning with page two if you prefer, one-half inch from the top (the text of your essay should begin one inch from the top), place a header with your last name, a space, and the page number. In most word-processing programs, you can do this from the "View" menu by selecting "Header and Footer." [NOTE: This is not shown in these models, but should be done in your own essays.] You should have one-inch margins on the right, the left, and the bottom of your page, and your essay should be double-spaced (set line spacing in your word processing program—do *not* place a hard return at the end of each line). Use one space at the end of terminal punctuation.

When you quote poetry, if the quotation is three or fewer lines, fit it right into your text. For instance, if I want to let you know that Blake begins "The Ecchoing Green" by juxtaposing "merry bells [that] ring / To welcome the spring" and "The sky-lark and thrush, / The birds of the bush," I would do it like I just did it. I might also note that Blake emphasizes this juxtaposition by the rhyme of "ring" and "sing," a rhyme that helps connect the natural and the human worlds because the sound describing the voices of the birds in the green echoes the sound describing the voice of human-made bells.

Notice that I keep the punctuation and the upper-case letters as they are in the poem. If I want to add something to make the quotation fit the grammar of my sentence, I do so by indicating the addition with brackets. If I wanted to leave something out of the poem and pick up the quotation a few words later, I would use ellipses, which are three dots with spaces between them (. . .).

I might then want to point out that, while "Old John" chimes in to the "merry" sounds as he "laugh[s] away care," the second stanza of the poem suggests his aging, and thus his experience of life, which might subtly trouble the innocence of the green. To show my point, I might quote the first five lines of the second stanza, though I might then find myself drifting from the close attention required in a solid analysis. If I take that chance of inattention, I would indent each line ten spaces and reproduce the lines of the poem just as they appear in the text. I would do this because I am quoting four or more lines of poetry. So the quotation would look like this:

> Old John with white hair
>
> Does laugh away care,
>
> Sitting under the oak,
>
> Among the old folk.
>
> They laugh at our play, . . .

After this, I had better make some particular observations about the language of the excerpt that I just quoted.

Remember, your essay's title is not the same as the title of the work you discuss in the essay. Your title has no quotation marks unless you have a quotation in it; neither is it underlined. Use quotation marks for the title of a short poem, essay, or short story. Italicize (or underline) the title of a book, a play, or a long poem—Wordsworth's *Prelude*, for instance.

In quoting prose, if the quotation takes up more than three lines of your text, you should indent the entire block ten spaces. Do not use ellipses (three periods separated by spaces) at the beginning or the end of the quotation; use them in the middle of the quotation to indicate you have removed words that are not essential to your point. Be sure to introduce all quotations with appropriate tags, blending quotations into your own sentence structure, grammar, and syntax. Punctuate quotations and cite page numbers as I do in the following sentence: DuBois begins his essay by depicting and defining the internalized "contempt and pity" of African-American "double-consciousness" (38); he ends the essay by turning that contempt and pity back upon the white America, a "dusty desert of dollars and smartness" (43). Notice that the end punctuation follows the page citation and is not within the quotation itself. Notice also that only the page number is within the parentheses. I would include an author's name only if the particular author was not clear from context.

If you have further questions about MLA style, look in the library for a copy of the *MLA Handbook for Writers of Research Papers,* use a writing handbook such as the Excellence in Literature *Handbook for Writers*, or visit the website below.

https://owl.english.purdue.edu/owl/resource/747/01/

Note: *This sample essay was provided courtesy of Dr. Robert Grotjohn, Professor Emeritus of English, Mary Baldwin College. It was one of the most helpful documents I received while in college, and I used it as a model for nearly every essay I wrote. I hope you find it equally helpful.*

How to Evaluate Writing

Let your speech be always with grace . . .

—Colossians 4:6

A constructive evaluation measures the student's work against an objective standard and assesses where and how the work meets or exceeds the standard, and what needs improvement. Always remember to evaluate skills from high to low, evaluating Content standards (Ideas/Concepts and Organization) first, then Style standards (Voice, Sentence Fluency, and Word Choice), and finally, Mechanics (Conventions and Presentation).

If a student has many significant areas of difficulty, evaluate only the skills that have been specifically taught. Be sure the student knows how to consult a writer's handbook and the formats and models in this guide for questions of structure, style, or usage. Use the numbered sections in the handbook, along with the rubric, to provide constructive, instructional feedback. Even students who begin the year with difficulty tend to catch up as they progress through the course and learn by repeatedly going through the read/think/write/evaluate/revise/evaluate cycle throughout the year.

How to Use a Writer's Handbook for Instructive Evaluation

A good writer's handbook makes it easy to offer specific, constructive feedback. If you have used a handbook such as *Writers INC* or the Excellence in Literature *Handbook for Writers*, you know that information is categorized into numbered paragraphs. These numbers allow you to direct the student to exactly the instruction he or she needs to fix an error or improve a skill.

For example, if your student is having difficulty with subject/verb agreement, you would look in the table of contents of the *Handbook for Writers* and find that subject/verb agreement appears in section 1.8 on page 242. On the student's paper, note the section number so that the student can visit the handbook, read the paragraph, look at the examples, and see how to correct the error. It is quick and efficient, and best of all, much more helpful than just telling the student to be sure that the subject and verb agree.

How to Evaluate the First Draft

After you do an initial read-through of the student's rough draft, get your writer's handbook and a copy of the rubric and evaluate the two Content skills, Ideas and Concepts and Organization.

I realize it is counter-intuitive for many parents to evaluate only the Content standards, because you will see mechanical errors or style problems in the rough draft. However, until the content and organization of the piece are finalized, there is little point in tweaking word choice or sentence fluency. Working only with content helps keep attention on the first draft priorities of ideas and organization, and avoids the distraction of too much red ink.

How to Evaluate a Final Draft

When you receive a revised draft, read through it quickly to gain an overall impression. Have the changes you discussed in the previous draft been satisfactorily made? Use a fresh copy of the rubric to assess each of the seven skill areas and provide a feedback number or symbol for each characteristic listed.

For each draft, return the student's paper with a filled-out rubric, a brief note highlighting the positive and negative things you noticed about the paper, and handbook section numbers so the student can look up challenging items.

Should You Require More than Two Drafts?

Two drafts—a first and a final—are all I recommend. Writing skills improve with each new assignment, and moving through the assignments in a timely manner ensures that students will not get bogged down and end up disliking one of the classics.

This section adapted from *Evaluate Writing the Easy Way* by Janice Campbell.

Excellence in Literature Evaluation Rubric

Name: Assignment:	Date: Evaluator:
Content: Ideas and Concepts _ The essay contains a strong, easily identified thesis. _ Interesting ideas and a compelling perspective hold the reader's attention. _ Relevant anecdotes, appropriate quotes, and specific details support the writer's position and demonstrate understanding of the prompt.	**Content: Organization** _ The structure of the paper enhances the presentation of the thesis and supporting ideas. _ Clear transitions move the reader easily from idea to idea. _ Quotes and textual support are blended smoothly, with correct tenses and formatting.
Style: Voice _ The writer speaks directly to the reader, using an appropriate tone and level of formality. _ The writer's voice is individual and engaging, providing a sense of the writer's personality. _ The writer demonstrates awareness of and respect for the audience and purpose of the writing.	**Mechanics: Conventions** _ Standard writing conventions (spelling, punctuation, capitalization, grammar, usage, paragraphing) are observed. _ Citations are correctly formatted using the MLA standard. _ Mechanical or typographical errors are few; only minor touch-ups needed.
Style: Sentence Fluency _ Sentences flow easily with graceful transitions. _ Sentences have a pleasant, appropriate rhythm and cadence when read aloud. _ Sentence structure is varied, with appropriate use of simple, complex, and compound sentences.	**Mechanics: Presentation** _ Essay is in MLA format: Times-New Roman font, 12 pt., 1" margins. _ Paper header with student, class, instructor, and date included. _ Essay prompt included after header and before title. _ Single space following all terminal punctuation.
Style: Word Choice _ Chosen words clearly convey the intended message. _ The words used are precise, interesting, powerful, engaging, and natural. _ The vocabulary is vivid and varied, though not necessarily exotic.	**Comments and Handbook Lookups**

Rating Scale
5 or + indicates that your essay demonstrated outstanding mastery in this area. 4 indicates that the essay is above average. 3 or = indicates that your essay was average and met assignment expectations in this area. 2 indicates that your essay was below average in this area. 1 or - indicates that you should write down this skill as a goal area for improvement.

Excellence in Literature: Reading and Writing through the Classics

Glossary

Allegory: A story in which ideas are represented or personified as actions, people, or things. Example: *Pilgrim's Progress* by John Bunyan.

Alliteration: The repetition of beginning consonant sounds through a sequence of words. Gerard Manley Hopkins is noted for using alliteration in lines such as "Fresh-firecoal chestnut-falls; finches' wings;" from "Pied Beauty."

Allude/Allusion: To make a reference, either implied or stated, to the Bible, mythology, literature, art, music, or history that relies on the reader's familiarity with the alluded-to work to make or reinforce a point in the current work.

Analogy: A comparison based upon similarities and relationships of things that are somewhat alike but mostly different. An analogy often makes a point-by-point comparison from a familiar object to an unfamiliar.

Antagonist: The character who opposes the main character (the protagonist).

Antithesis: A counter-proposition that denotes a direct contrast to the original proposition, balancing an argument for parallel structure.

Archetype: A plot pattern, such as the quest or the redeemer/scapegoat, or character element, such as the cruel stepmother, that recurs across cultures.

Assonance: The repetition of vowel sounds in a series of words. Example: "The rain in Spain falls mainly on the plain" from *Pygmalion* by George Bernard Shaw.

Ballad: A narrative poem or song with a repeating refrain. A ballad often tells the story of a historical event or retells a folk legend. Example: "The Raven" by Edgar Allen Poe.

Beast Fable: Also known as a "beast epic," this is an often satirical, allegorical style in which the main characters are animals. It is often written as a mock epic. Example: *Animal Farm* by George Orwell.

Blank Verse: Unrhymed poetry, usually iambic pentameter.

Burlesque: Refers to ridiculous exaggeration in language, usually one that makes the discrepancy between the words and the situation or the character silly. For example, to have a king speak like an idiot or a workman speak like a king (especially, say, in blank verse) is burlesque. Similarly, a very serious situation can be burlesqued by having the characters in it speak or behave in ridiculously inappropriate ways. In other words, burlesque creates a large gap between the situation or the characters and the style with which they speak or act out the event.

Caricature: The technique of exaggerating for comic and satiric effect one particular feature of a subject, in order to achieve a grotesque or ridiculous effect. Caricatures can be created either through words or pictures.

Characterization: The artistic presentation of a fictional character.

Citation: A standardized reference to a source of information in a written work. The citation usually includes author, title, publisher, and so forth, in a specific format. In the MLA style of citation that we use with this curriculum, the citations appear as signal phrases in the body of the text, and a "works cited" list follows the text.

Climax: The turning point in fiction; the transition from rising to falling action.

Comedy: In literary terms a comedy is a story, often centered on love, that has a positive ending. It may or may not be humorous.

Conflict: A struggle between two opposing forces. The conflict usually forms the central drama in a fictional narrative, and can be man vs. man, man vs. God, man vs. nature, man vs. society, or even man vs. himself.

Consonance: An "almost rhyme" in which consonants agree, but the vowels that precede them differ. Example: word/lord, slip/slop.

Couplet: In poetry, a pair of rhyming lines often appearing at the end of a sonnet.

Denouement: Resolution or conclusion.

Diction: An author's word choices.

Didactic: Literature with a moralistic or instructive purpose.

Elegy: A poem, usually written as a formal lament on the death of a person. In classical time an elegy was any poem written in elegiac meter. Example: "In Memory of W. B. Yeats" by W. H. Auden.

End Rhyme: The repetition of identical or similar sounds in two or more different words found at the end of poetic lines.

Epic: A long narrative poem that tells a story, usually about the deeds of a hero. Example: Beowulf.

Epigram: A brief saying or poem, often ironic or satirical.

Epigraph: A phrase, quotation, or poem that suggests something about the theme and is set at the beginning of a chapter or book.

Epistolary Style: A novel composed of a series of letters.

Essay: A paper that takes a position on a topic.

Euphemism: The substitution of a socially acceptable word or expression in place of harsh or unacceptable language. Example: "Passed away" for "died."

Exposition: The part of the narrative structure in which the scene is set, characters introduced, and the situation established. It usually falls at the beginning of the book, but additional exposition is often scattered throughout the work.

Fable: A short story, usually featuring animals or other non-human characters, that illustrates a moral lesson. Example: Aesop's "The Crow and the Pitcher."

Falling Action: The portion of plot structure, usually following the climax, in which the problems encountered during the rising action are solved.

Figure of Speech: A comparison in which something is pictured or figured in other more familiar terms. See simile and metaphor.

Flashback: A plot device in which a scene from the fictional past is brought into the fictional present, often to explain or illustrate a character's next action.

Foot: A group of syllables that form a basic unit of poetic rhythm.

Foreshadow: Hints or clues about future events in a narrative.

Framed Narrative: A story or stories told within a narrative frame. Example: *The Canterbury Tales* by Geoffrey Chaucer. Chaucer has framed a vivid grouping of stories within the frame of a narrative about a group of pilgrims who are traveling to Canterbury.

Free Verse: Poetry that does not rhyme, has no set line length, and is not set to traditional meter.

Full Stop: A period or other punctuation mark that indicates the end of a sentence.

Genre: A category of classification for literature such as fiction, non-fiction, and so forth. Pronounced zhahn-ruh.

Gothic Novel: A genre that evokes an aura of mystery and may include ghosts, dark and stormy nights, isolated castles, and supernatural happenings. Example: *Wuthering Heights* by Emily Brontë or *Frankenstein* by Mary Shelley.

Handbook: A writer's handbook such as the *Handbook for Writers* from Excellence in Literature, *Write for College, Writer's Inc.* from Write Source, or *Writer's Reference* by Diana Hacker.

Heroic Couplet: Two rhymed lines in iambic pentameter, forming a complete thought. This form was often used by Alexander Pope.

Homonym/Homophone: Words that sound much the same but have different meanings, origins, or spelling.

Hubris: A term derived from the Greek language that means excessive pride. In Greek tragedy and mythology, hubris often leads to the hero's downfall.

Hyperbole: Overstatement through exaggerated language.

Imagery: Words, phrases, and sensory details used to create a mood or mental picture in a reader's mind. Example: From "Mariana" by Alfred, Lord Tennyson:
"With blackest moss the flower-plots
Were thickly crusted, one and all;
The rusted nails fell from the knots
That held the pear to the gable wall.
The broken sheds looked sad and strange:
Unlifted was the clinking latch;
Weeded and worth the ancient thatch

Excellence in Literature: Reading and Writing through the Classics

Upon the lonely moated grange . . . ”

Iambic Pentameter: In poetry, a metrical pattern in a ten-syllable line of verse in which five unaccented syllables alternate with five accented syllables, with the accent usually falling on the second of each pair of syllables.

Irony: A stylistic device or figure of speech in which the real meaning of the words is different from (and opposite to) the literal meaning. Irony, unlike sarcasm, tends to be ambiguous, bringing two contrasting meanings into play.

Manners: A novel of manners focuses on and describes in detail the social customs and habits of a particular social group. Examples include *Pride and Prejudice* by Jane Austen and *Age of Innocence* by Edith Wharton.

Metaphor: A comparison between two objects, not using the terms “like” or “as.”

Meter: The pattern of stressed and unstressed syllables in a line of poetry.

Mock Heroic: A satiric style which sets up a deliberately disproportionate and witty distance between the elevated language used to describe an action or event and the triviality or foolishness of the action (using, for example, the language of epics to describe a tea party). The mock heroic style tends to be an inside joke, in that it appeals to the sophistication of a reader familiar with the epic original but is not understood by readers who are not familiar with the traditional epic form. It encourages the reader to see the ridiculousness of the heroic pretensions of trivial people and is thus an excellent vehicle for skewering the sin of pride. Example: “Mac Flecknoe” by John Dryden or Pope’s “Rape of the Lock.”

Motif: A recurrent device, formula, or situation, often connecting a fresh idea with common patterns of existing thought.

Myth: A type of story that is usually symbolic and extensive, including stories shared across a culture to explain its history and traditions. Example: “Romulus and Remus.”

Narrator: The character who tells the story. This may or may not be the hero, and the narrator may be reliable or unreliable. Example: Ishmael in *Moby Dick*.

Nature: As it refers to a person, this is used to identify something inborn or inherent, such as the “old nature” of Scripture, that often leads to predictable actions.

Octave: In poetry, the first eight lines of the Italian, or Petrarchan, sonnet.

Ode: A lyric poem with a serious topic and formal tone but without formal pattern. This form was especially popular among the Romantic poets. Example: "Ode to the West Wind" by Percy Bysshe Shelley.

Omniscient Point of View: In literature, a narrative perspective from multiple points of view that gives the reader access to the thoughts of all the characters.

Onomatopoeia: The formation or use of a word that sounds like what it means. Example: hiss; sizzle; pop.

Oxymoron: A figure of speech that combines two seemingly contradictory elements. Example: living death; sweet sorrow.

Parable: A short story with an explicit moral lesson. Example: The parable of the sower (Matthew 13:18–30).

Paradox: A statement that may appear contradictory but is actually true. Example: "Less is more."

Parody: A style of writing that deliberately seeks to ridicule another style, primarily through exaggeration.

Pastoral: Poem or play that describes an idealized, simple life that country folk, usually shepherds, are imagined to live in a world full of beauty, music, and love.

Personification: To endow a non-human object with human qualities. Example: Death in "Death Be Not Proud" by John Donne.

Picaresque: A style of novel that features a loosely connected series of events, rather than a tightly constructed plot, often with a non-traditional hero. Example: *Moll Flanders* by Daniel Defoe.

Plagiarism: To plagiarize is to copy or borrow the work or ideas of another author without acknowledgment. It is both unethical and illegal. When you are writing anything, such as essays, reports, dissertations, or creative works, you must cite your sources of information, including books, periodicals, or online resources, within your text as well as in a list of references appended to the work.

Plot: The sequence of narrated events that form a story.

Poetic Justice: A literary device in which virtue is ultimately rewarded or vice punished.

Point of View: The perspective from which people, events, and other details in a story are viewed.

Protagonist: The main character in a work, either male or female.

Pseudonym: A false name used to disguise a writer's identity. Example: Mary Anne Evans used the pseudonym George Eliot.

Pun: A wordplay that exploits the double meaning or ambiguity in a word to create an amusing effect. Example: The title of *The Importance of Being Earnest* by Oscar Wilde.

Quest: A type of literary plot that focuses on a protagonist's journey toward a difficult goal. There may or may not be a physical journey involved. Example: Homer's *Odyssey*; J. R. R. Tolkien's *The Lord of the Rings*.

Realism: A type of literature that tries to present life as it really is.

Reductio ad absurdum: A popular satiric technique in which the author agrees enthusiastically with the basic attitudes or assumptions he wishes to satirize and, by pushing them to a logically ridiculous extreme, exposes the foolishness of the original attitudes and assumptions. Example: "A Modest Proposal" by Jonathan Swift.

Refrain: A phrase, line, or group of lines that is repeated throughout a poem, usually after every stanza.

Resolution: The point of closure to the conflict in the plot.

Rhetoric: The art of using language to persuade or influence others. Sometimes includes the idea of eloquence (an older meaning) or of insincerity or artificiality in language (more modern interpretation). Examples: Mark Antony's speech in *Julius Caesar* by William Shakespeare or the character of Squealer in *Animal Farm* by George Orwell.

Rhyme Scheme: The pattern of end rhymes in a poem, noted by small letters, e.g., abab or abcba, etc.

Rising Action: The part of the plot structure in which events complicate or intensify the conflict, or introduce additional conflict.

Romance: A type of novel that presents an idealized picture of life. A novel of romance can be considered almost the opposite of a novel of realism. If you were expecting that the definition of "romance" would have something to do with love, you may want to look at the definition of "comedy" instead.

Rubric: A checklist for scoring that includes guidelines for expectations.

Sarcasm: A form of verbal irony in which apparent praise is actually criticism. Example: "A modest little person, with much to be modest about." Winston Churchill

Satire: A composition in verse or prose that uses humor, irony, sarcasm, or ridicule to point out vice or folly in order to expose, discourage, and change morally offensive attitudes or behaviors. It has been aptly described as an attack with a smile. Example: "A Modest Proposal" by Jonathan Swift.

Scansion: The process of analytically scanning a poem line by line to determine its meter.

Setting: The time and place in which the action of a story, poem, or play takes place.

Simile: A comparison of two things, using the words "like" or "as." Example: "My love is like a red, red rose . . . " by Robert Burns.

Soliloquy: A monologue in which a character talks to himself. Example: Hamlet's "To be or not to be . . . " soliloquy.

Sonnet: A fixed verse form consisting of fourteen lines, usually in iambic pentameter. Variations include Italian (Petrarchan), Shakespearean, and Spenserian.

Stanza: A section of a poem, preceded and followed by an extra line space.

Stereotype: A characterization based on the assumption that a personal trait such as gender, age, ethnic or national identity, religion, occupation, or marital status is predictably accompanied by certain characteristics, actions, even values.

Stock Character: A flat character sketch that fills a classic, easily understood role without much detail. Example: The wicked stepmother in *Cinderella*.

Stream of Consciousness: A modern writing style that replicates and records the random flow of thoughts, emotions, memories, and associations as they rush through a character's mind. Example: *To the Lighthouse* by Virginia Woolf.

Structure: The arrangement of the various elements in a work.

Style: A distinctive manner of expression distinguished by the writer's diction, rhythm, imagery, and so on.

Syllabus: An outline of course requirements. In *Excellence in Literature*, the syllabus is this book in its entirety.

Symbol: A person, place, thing, event, or pattern in a literary work that is not only itself but also stands for something else, often something more abstract. Common symbolism includes darkness as a representation of confusion or evil; a storm as foreboding or a threat; or beauty as a symbol of virtue. This PDF may help you understand symbols: http://goo.gl/gGLU4O

Textual Support: Brief quotes from a text that is being analyzed. These quotes should usually be smoothly integrated into an original, analytical sentence.

Theme: The main idea or dominant concern of a novel, play, or poem stated in a generalized, abstract way. Example: "Crime does not pay." "Honesty is the best policy."

Tone: The attitude a novel or poem takes toward its subject.

Tragedy: A story in which the character begins at a high point but ends badly, often because of a fatal flaw in his character that causes him to make poor choices. Example: *King Lear* by William Shakespeare; *Oedipus Rex* by Sophocles.

Tragic Flaw: An error in judgment, accidental wrongdoing, or unwitting mistake that results in tragedy, derived from the Greek idea of *hamartia*, or missing the mark.

Tragic Hero: A character, often a noble person of high rank, who comes to a disastrous end in his or her confrontation with a superior force (fortune, the gods, social forces, universal values), but also comes to understand the meaning of his or her deeds and to accept an appropriate punishment.

Unreliable Narrator: A speaker or voice whose narration is consciously or unconsciously deceiving. This type of narration is often subtly undermined by details in the story or through inconsistencies with general knowledge.

Voice: The style, personality, and tone of a narrative; also the speaker or narrator. An appropriate voice captures the correct level of formality, social distance, and personality for the purpose of the writing and the audience.

Writer's Handbook: See *handbook*.

Selected Resources

There is an endless supply of books on reading, writing, and literature, but it can be difficult to find the best. As I look at my bookshelves, I see that many books boast an array of sticky-note flags. When I open them, I find extensive marginal notations, underlined passages, and occasionally, extra slips of paper left at especially important spots. Here are just a few of the most-thumbed volumes on my bookshelves, as well as a few e-resources you will find helpful.

Adventures in Art by David and Shirley Quine- This interactive e-text is designed to help you "visualize the significant changes in ideas throughout history, and then relate those changes to their cultural meaning." This is an excellent art and worldview context supplement to EIL.

American Passages: A Literary Survey- This well-organized site, designed to enhance the study of American literature, offers timelines, art, and other context information in an easily navigated format. One unique feature allows students to construct a multimedia slideshow of selected materials from the site; then use the slideshow for a presentation.

http://www.learner.org/amerpass/index.html

"Analyzing Poetry" from Study Guide-

http://www.studyguide.org/poetry_tips.htm

Benét's Reader's Encyclopedia- This wonderful resource is described as "the classic and only encyclopedia of world literature in a single volume including poets, playwrights, novelists, and belletrists, synopses, historical data, major characters, in literature, myths and legends, literary terms, artistic movements, and prize winners." Any of the older editions will include the important elements of the Western literary tradition. I use it often.

The Company of the Creative: A Christian Reader's Guide to Great Literature and Its Themes by David L. Larson- This helpful guide offers brief overviews of great authors and their work, plus useful recommendations for further reading.

Developing Linguistic Patterns Through Poetry Memorization by Andrew Pudewa– To write well, a student needs to internalize the rhythm and cadence of well-composed language. This book will help you accomplish that.

A Dictionary of Literary Symbols by Michael Ferber- This helpful guide, now available free online, "explains . . . literary symbols that we all frequently encounter (such as swan, rose, moon, gold), and gives hundreds of cross-references and quotations" from classic authors, the Bible, and English, American, and European literature.

http://www.academia.edu/1052805/A_DICTIONARY_OF_LITERARY_SYMBOLS_By_Michael_Ferber

Discovering Music- Dr. Carol Reynolds has created a "unique curriculum [that] takes you through the history of music, the arts, and Western Culture from 1600 to 1914" in about 13 hours of video instruction. This is an excellent context supplement to EIL. http://discoveringmusic.net/

The Elegant Essay Writing Lessons: Building Blocks for Analytical Writing by Lesha Myers- An elegantly simple introduction to essay writing, organized in units. This may be used before or concurrently with Excellence in Literature.

Excellence-in-Literature.com- Here you will find many of the context resources and study references used in the *Excellence in Literature* curriculum and *Classics-Based Writing.*

Excellence in Literature Handbook for Writers- The first half of this 400+ page handbook for student and teacher contains detailed instruction on essay writing, including a selection of sample outlines for different types of papers. The second half is a guide to usage and style, including sentence construction, word usage, punctuation, and more.

Gutenberg: Free Books- This wonderful site contains many classic books in downloadable formats. I do not recommend reading extensively on the computer screen, but these book files can be useful when you cannot find a copy locally.

How to Read a Book: The Classic Guide to Intelligent Reading by Mortimer J. Adler and Charles Van Doren- There are multiple levels of reading—elementary, inspectional, and synoptical—and the authors clearly explain each and teach the reader how to appropriately read various types of literature.

How to Read and Why by Harold Bloom- A Yale professor and author of many books on literature, Bloom offers this brief volume of selections chosen not "as an exclusive list of what to read, but rather a sampling of works that best illustrate why to read." For a more extensive overview of the classics, you may want to read The Western Canon.

How to Read Literature Like a Professor: A Lively and Entertaining Guide to Reading Between the Lines by Thomas C. Foster- This light-hearted guide offers a very accessible look at the themes and symbols found under the surface in great literature.

How to Read Slowly: Reading for Comprehension by James W. Sire- Sire, the author of the Christian worldview classic, *The Universe Next Door*, has written an excellent, concise introduction (just six chapters!) to reading literature from a worldview perspective.

Imitations in Writing: The Grammar of Poetry by Matt Whiting- This accessible text "focuses on teaching the fundamentals of poetry (figurative language, meter, rhyme, etc.) by means of imitation and review." We found it to be a very easy-to-use introduction to poetry.

Invitation to the Classics: A Guide to Books You have Always Wanted to Read by Louise Cowan and Os Guinness- This attractive guide presents a chronological survey of great literature. The purpose of the book is to "introduce the Western literary masterworks in a clear and simple style that is mature in seriousness and tone and Christian in perspective—and in doing so, to help reawaken Western people to the vibrant heritage of these classics that are rich in themselves and in their two-thousand-year relationship to the Christian faith."

Librivox: Free Audio Books- The exciting thing about LibriVox is that you do not have to be content with just the books they offer—you can record and upload your own! The quality of these amateur recordings varies, but the price is right. http://librivox.org/

The Lifetime Reading Plan by Clifton Fadiman- Fadiman offers an overview of the Western canon, with brief discussions about each author and his or her greatest works. His aim is to help the reader "avoid mental bankruptcy" and to "understand something …of our position in space and time …[and] know how we got the ideas by which …we live."

Norton Anthologies: I recommend looking for used copies of the Norton Anthologies at used bookstores, remainder tables, or online, because they contain extremely reliable, high-quality author introductions and their chronological format makes it easy to see the literary context of the works we will study throughout Excellence in Literature. Other anthologies may be useful, but I like the Norton editions because they tend to stick with the classics, especially in older editions. I suggest getting the American, English, World, and Poetry anthologies.

Norton Literature Online- The W. W. Norton sites, home of the renowned Norton Anthologies, offer a wealth of nicely organized context information, a few audio resources, plus a valuable introduction to writing about literature which includes a glossary, flashcards, and quizzes. Highly recommended. Access the StudySpace for the book you need through http://books.wwnorton.com/studyspace/disciplines/literature.aspx?DiscId=7 or go directly to your area of interest.

http://www.wwnorton.com/college/english/literature/OpenSite.htm

American Literature- www.wwnorton.com/college/english/naal7/

British Literature- http://www.wwnorton.com/college/english/nael/

World Literature- http://www.wwnorton.com/college/english/literature/nawol.htm

Writing About Literature: Norton's basic instruction in how to read analytically and write an analytical essay. This resource seems to move regularly. If this link does not work, try doing a web search for "Writing About Literature: Norton," and you may find it.

http://www.wwnorton.com/college/english/litweb10/writing/welcome.aspx

On Writing Well: An Informal Guide to Writing Nonfiction by William Zinsser-
There is a good reason that this classic resource just celebrated its thirtieth anniversary with a new edition; it is an excellent model for its subject. Zinsser begins with an overview of writing principles, then moves into detailed discussion of forms and methods. It is a valuable resource for any writer.

The Politically Incorrect Guide to English and American Literature by Elizabeth Kantor, Ph.D. is a delightful romp through selected English language literature. It begins by pointing out that "the greatest English literature is explicitly Christian and celebrates military courage," and goes on to explain why dead white males deserve the respect they have traditionally received. Overall, the book provides a memorable introduction to the ideas that have shaped the literary world, as well as sound recommendations for books you must not miss (most of them are included in the Excellence in Literature series).

Reading Between the Lines: A Christian Guide to Literature by Gene Edward Veith, Jr.- This fascinating guide begins with a chapter on the importance of reading, then progresses through the forms, modes, and traditions of literature, with extensive end-notes for each chapter. It is a book that is worth reading and rereading, for each time you do, you will glean new insights.

Teaching the Classics: A Socratic Method for Literary Education with Worldview Supplement by Adam Andrews (DVDs and manual)- This would be an excellent course to view during middle school, as well as a few times while working through the Excellence in Literature series. The Socratic method of thinking is applicable to other disciplines as well, and can be an enormous help through the high school and college years.

Vocabulary Study: I like Dynamic Literacy's W*ord Build* program, which goes beyond the simple study of roots by using "morphology, the study of the units of meaning in words. [Just as] mastery of phonics helps students 'sound out' unfamiliar words; a mastery of morphics helps students 'mean out' unfamiliar words." An alternative is the Vocabulary from Classical Roots series, which presents Greek and Latin roots in a series of well-designed lessons.

Write for College: A Student Handbook- Specific instructions on many types of writing, plus a proofreader's guide to grammar, punctuation, and style, and much more. Younger students may prefer *Writer's INC*, which is similar, but for

11th–12th grades and beyond, *Write for College* or the EIL *Handbook for Writers* (referenced earlier) is most useful.

A Writer's Reference by Diana Hacker- I often turn to this brief handbook because of its handy tabbed format and helpful citation guides, including MLA and APA styles. It would be a useful supplement to either of the other suggested guides.

Word Processing Software

If you do not have a full-featured word processing program such as Microsoft Word, I recommend Google's free online suite of applications, including a word processor, spreadsheet program, and other tools. All you need for access to these is a free Google account, available at https://accounts.google.com/SignUp?.

A second option would be to download OpenOffice, a free, open-source suite of office productivity software. It is available at http://www.openoffice.org.

About the Author

Janice Campbell and her husband Donald homeschooled their sons from preschool into early college using a lifestyle of learning approach influenced by Charlotte Mason, classical learning, and the Thomas Jefferson method. Her books and resources reflect Janice's focus on twaddle-free, active learning (she did have boys, after all!).

Janice speaks at conferences nationwide on subjects including literature, writing, high school records and transcripts, as well as micro-business and multiple streams of income for homeschool families. She graduated *cum laude* from Mary Baldwin College with a B.A. in English and is the author of the *Excellence in Literature* curriculum for grades 8-12, *Transcripts Made Easy*, and *Get a Jump Start on College*, and publisher of a new edition of the 1857 McGuffey Readers with instructions for use with Charlotte Mason methods. She is also Director of the National Association of Independent Writers and Editors (NAIWE).

Whether teaching high school students to love literature or writers and entrepreneurs how to create multiple streams of income, Janice's focus is on lighting lamps so that others can more easily find their way. Her website, www.Everyday-Education.com, offers inspiration, resources, and a free e-newsletter.

2014 Everyday Education Book List

Here is our 2014 book list. You'll always find the most current information and instant ordering, as well as e-books and new items, at www.Everyday-Education.com, but this will give you an idea of what is currently available. You may pay with cash or credit/debit card, or make checks payable to Everyday Education, LLC. Thank you!

Quantity	Item	Print Book	With ebook	Total
	Excellence in Literature: www.Excellence-in-Literature.com			
	English I: Introduction to Literature	$29	$39	
	English II: Lit & Composition	$29	$39	
	English III: American Literature	$29	$39	
	English IV: British Literature	$29	$39	
	English V: World Literature	$29	$39	
	—Complete Curriculum (1-5 in books or a binder- circle selection)	$139	$189	
	Handbook for Writers	$39	$49	
	TimeFrame: The Twaddle-Free Timeline- one copy	$19	$29	
	—SAVE! TimeFrame: 2 for $35; 3 or more for $15 each		N/A	
	1857 McGuffey Readers: www.1857McGuffey.com			
	First Reader	9.99	N/A	
	Second Reader	10.99	N/A	
	Third Reader	11.99	N/A	
	—SAVE! Set of Readers 1, 2, and 3	$29	N/A	
	Fourth Reader	11.99	N/A	
	Fifth Reader	12.99	N/A	
	Sixth Reader	13.99	N/A	
	— SAVE! Set of Readers 4, 5, and 6	$35	N/A	
	—SAVE! Set of all six Readers	$60	N/A	
	Other Resources: www.Everyday-Education.com			
	Transcripts Made Easy	$22	$29	
	Get a Jump Start on College	$12	$19	
	—SAVE! High School Success bundle- Transcripts/Jump Start (save $8)	$29	$39	
	Grammar Made Easy by Connie Schenkelberg	$29	$39	
	Spelling Made Easy (Ungraded/ 2 years of lessons)	$39	$49	
	—SAVE! Language Arts bundle- GME, SME	$60	$80	
	Elegant Essay by Lesha Myers: Teacher's Manual and Student Book	$49	N/A	
	Elegant Essay: Student Book only	$29	N/A	
	Evaluate Writing the Easy Way	$5	$7	
	—SAVE! EIL Extras bundle- Handbook, Elegant Essay, Timeline	$70	N/A	

NOTE: Getting the e-book along with the print book allows each of your students to follow along and use the text online. xFor Excellence in Literature, this means they can click live inks (on most computer systems) instead of typing in URLs. (This option is for use within a single immediate family only.)

Quantity	Item	Print Book	With ebook	Total	
Microbusiness and Math					
	SAVE! Microbusiness Curriculum by Carol Topp, CPA– 4 Book	$39	N/A		
	SAVE! Chenier's Practical Math Dictionary and Application Guide ($27.95 ea.)	$49	N/A		
Ship to:	Name				
	Address				
	City, State, Zip				
	E-mail	Phone			

Everyday Education, LLC, P.O. Box 549, Ashland, VA 23005
www.Everyday-Education.com || janice@eilit.com